Felton Hawkins

Building a Great House

Overcoming the Ordinary to Possess God's Extraordinary

Building a Great House:
Overcoming Life's Ordinary to Possess God's Extraordinary
ISBN: 0-9721623-1-3
Library of Congress Control Number: 2005905485

Publication Date: November 2005

Unless otherwise noted, Scripture quotations are taken from the King James Version of the Holy Bible.

Copyright © 2005 by Felton Hawkins
Cover design: Brennan Crick
Text Design: Red Letter Writing Service

Published by Empowered for Impact
for Full Gospel Kingdom Church
PO Box 742
Newport News, VA 23607

All rights reserved.
This book, or parts thereof, may not be reproduced in any form without permission from the author and or publisher.

Printed in the United States of America

10 9 8 7 6 5 4

Printed in the United States by Morris Publishing
3212 East Highway 30
Kearney, NE 68847
1-800-650-7888

Dedication

I would like to dedicate this book to some very special people in my life:

To my mother, Roma Hawkins, who is the reason why I am here today;

To my loving wife, Sylvia, a great comfort and support to the ministry, the rock upon the rock that loves and supports me;

To my wonderful children, my firstborn Rafael, to Maurice, and last but not least, to little Miss Destinee;

To some of my greatest allies, my brothers and sisters, Gerald, Romane, Tina, and Eric;

And it goes without saying, to my church family, who has been one of the greatest blessings in my life. What a wonderful group of people, who assist me in fulfilling the will and purpose of God for my life!

"Building a Great House will not only inspire readers to expect more out of life, but it also provides the tools necessary to achieve bigger goals."
- *Stacey Seay, RAWSISTAZ.com*

"Powerful, highly motivating and life changing!"
- *Kimberly T. Matthews*
Contributing Author of *Journey to a Blissful Life*

"Building A Great House is an excellent blueprint for living as God ordained. [It is] a must read for anyone searching to understand His specific intentions for our lives."
- *Jacquelin Thomas,*
Author of *The Prodigal Husband* and *Saved In The City*

Building a Great House

Contents

Introduction

1.	God's Call to Greatness	1
2.	The Blueprint of a Great House	13
3.	The Foundation	29
4.	The Materials of a Great House	41
5.	Solomon Builds a Great House	51
6.	Committed to Building the House	63
7.	Reflecting God's Glory	83
8.	Recognizing God's Presence	97
9.	Characteristics of Great People	107
10.	A Living Tabernacle	127
11.	The Tabernacle Sacrificed	141
12.	Conclusion	151

Prayer of Salvation

Introduction

In life, we all learn that it is easy to be the norm and do what everybody else is doing just to survive as average. We often go with the crowd and take the "easy way" out. The easy way is just to try to get by while we're here on planet earth, and somehow make it to heaven the best we can, if we can. It is easy to be small, think small and never strive to do great things; however, it is critically important that Christians and non-Christians alike understand God's intent for their lives, and His desire for them to be great in every aspect. Once we really build a relationship with God, He begins to reveal His specific intentions for us. No matter what negative path life has led us down, it is necessary for us to know that before the foundation of the world, God's purpose and desire for our lives is that we excel.

Of course, there is a price to be paid; becoming great does not come easy. We must always remember that many times great people are birthed in circumstances that do not seem to be advantageous. Notice however, that where there is immeasurable faith and the power of God, God is able to raise up something great even out of the ashes. We must believe that God made us to be overcomers in His Kingdom. When we have God's word and His commitment to stand with us and bring us to that place of promise, then we know that, whatever it takes, we will achieve the goals that we desire and that He desires for us.

We all know that our lives are under construction. Many negative things are being torn down, and many wonderful things are being constructed, as we let the Holy Spirit build in us a great habitation, A Great House.

One

God's Call to Greatness

"Nevertheless, the foundation of God standeth sure, having this seal: The Lord knoweth them that are His, and let everyone that nameth the name of Christ depart from iniquity. But in a Great House, there are not only vessels of gold and silver but also of wood and earth. Some to honor and some to dishonor. If a man therefore purges himself from these, he shall be a vessel unto honor."

I Timothy 2:19-21

Did you know that God never called you to be a loser, but He designed and called you to be a champion? Anything that God does He does with greatness, and when God made you He made you to be great. He is always in the process of causing you to improve in every aspect of life. In everything you do, God wants you to excel. He wants you to think and dream big; He wants you to see yourself doing great things. We don't serve a trivial, pitiful or insufficient God; we serve a great big God with great miracle-working power. He is great and greatly to be praised. God is not average; He is excellent, so why shouldn't you be? Because God is great, and you come from God, He intends for you to be great.

In our personal, professional, spiritual and in every other aspect of our lives, we should all strive to be more than mediocre. Unfortunately, many people have rejected God's call to greatness; there are hundreds of thousands of people who have no aspirations to be anything more than ordinary. They are satisfied with being normal, and have decided to settle for whatever life hands them. They have no desire to excel or go above and beyond in any area, and are content with a life of mediocrity. Rather than being great, they embrace normality; they seem to prefer everything at an average standard. They like average cars, bank accounts, houses and even churches, and have no desire for anything more. God is not average, so why should His church be? Why should His people possess the mentality of mediocrity? Even if you start off with small beginnings, know that it isn't where God wants you to stay. More important than the way you start is how you finish. Your beginning may be that you have to accept the crumbs from the Master's table, but some of us have settled for only the crumbs in our lives thinking that it's the best we can do. Don't just settle for the crumbs. While the crumbs may have to do for now, strive to move on to the full course meal that the Master continually serves and wants you to partake in and enjoy.

> *Even if you start off with small beginnings, know that it isn't where God wants you to stay.*

�֍ Building a Great House �֍

Abraham is a perfect example of a man with small beginnings. He started out as a nobody, but became the father of many nations. Abraham was a heathen in the woods somewhere, dwelling among idol worshippers and had nothing going for himself. He didn't know anything; he possessed neither land nor wealth; he didn't know where his life was headed; he was walking around in a hole of darkness! But one day little old Abraham met a great God. When he met God, God spoke to Abraham these words:

> *"And I will make of thee a great nation, and I will bless thee, and make thy name great; and thou shalt be a blessing. And I will bless them that bless thee, and curse them that curseth thee: and in thee shall all families of the earth be blessed."*
>
> *Genesis 12:2-3*

God says to Abraham, "I am going to make you great." God already knew His plans concerning Abraham; He knew before He ever spoke those words to him, that His intent for his life was far above the life that Abraham was living when He and Abraham met. God makes a covenant with Abraham, and whenever God makes a covenant, it's because He wants to establish and accomplish something great. Though Abraham started with nothing, in the end, he was exceedingly and abundantly rich! He possessed wealth, had servants, and owned cattle and land. He had so much that the land he lived on was too small to allow his family and his nephew Lot's family to dwell peaceably!

God took this man from his beginning of not even being able to produce a single child to multiplying his seed so miraculously that it could not be numbered, like the stars in the heavens! He made it so that all of the families of the earth would be blessed because of Abraham.

In the same manner, God wants you to have a great family. Now, it's not necessary to have one hundred children to have a great family; your family should be great in quality regardless of its size. God doesn't want you to have just an everyday family life. He wants you to enjoy the family life you have and make it the very best it can be. If your family is mediocre, maybe it is because you, as the leader of your family, are mediocre. If your family's not going anywhere, perhaps it is because the head of the family is not leading the way. If God intends for you as an individual to be great, then He intends for your family to be great, as well.

> *If God intends for you as an individual to be great, then He intends for your family to be great, as well.*

He wants you to have a great professional life. Don't settle for a petty, run-of-the-mill job, where you're just getting by, living from paycheck to paycheck, and doing something that you hate. You despise getting up in the morning to go to work because your job confines and restricts you. It doesn't allow you to operate in your full potential and exercise your natural, God-given talent. Instead of growing in your passion and expanding in a career that you love, you feel as if you are going nowhere fast. You haven't had a promotion in five years and you haven't had a raise in ten. It's just the same old, same old, that puts just enough money in your pocket to keep you bound by debt. You have settled for a little job, saying to yourself, "I guess this is the best I can do," while the job barely allows your ends to meet. That is not what God wants for you. He wants you to have a great work experience and a great career. He wants you to excel in everything you do. He wants you to be the head and not the tail. He wants you to be on the top and not the bottom. Get rid of the mentality that keeps you in a place of mediocrity in your work place. Develop a mentality that will earn you the company instead. If not *that* company, *your own* company!

To be great, you must have a great spiritual life. God doesn't want any spiritual Tiny Tims, people who are small, weak and frail in the spirit. He wants some great folks! People who know how to cast out devils, people who know how to lay hands on themselves and recover from sickness and disease, people who know how to speak to the storm and tell the storm, "You'd better settle down,

> *Develop a mentality that will earn you the company; if not the company you work for, your own company!*

because greatness is coming through!" If the water's too high, have the faith to walk on it. If the wind's blowing too strongly, be able to speak to it. If a mountain gets in your way, be able to say "Mountain be thou removed," and know that you can do these things because you serve a great God. The devil can't stay in your house or in your life when you serve a great God. Sickness can't stay in your body and poverty can't stay in your pocket. Who can stand before you? Demons tremble when you call on that great name! Why? Because The Greater One lives on the inside!

Decide that you don't want a small spiritual life, but a great spiritual life instead.

You may even be facing trials today, but know that though your trials may be great, He who dwells in you is greater. Understand that the storms may be great, but the God inside of you is greater. Your family may be experiencing a crisis, but because God dwells in you, you're greater than that crisis. Remember that in I John 4:4, the Bible declares:

"Greater is He that is in you than He that is in the world."

You have to know that the fire may be hot, but the Spirit of God dwells in you and is able to overcome and quench that fire. God wants somebody who can go through the fire. God wants someone who can deal with adversity. God wants to have someone to brag on; He wants to have someone that He can say, "That's my son" or "That's my daughter" about. Can He say that about you? Not just because you look good, but because you've been able to go through a storm and come out victorious. Because you have proven that you can stand the test. He wants to be able to brag on you, not just because of where you are, but because of what you went through to get to where you are. The fact of the matter is, it's easy to achieve something and get somewhere when you don't experience any opposition on the way; you haven't had to overcome anything! When you are able to pursue and

> *When you are able to pursue and accomplish greatness even in the face of trials, then God will be able to brag on you.*

accomplish greatness even in the face of trials, then God will be able to brag on you and say, "That's my *boy* right there; that's *my* girl right there!"

Look at how God was able to brag on Job. Job was rich and living in abundance when he met the most horrific trial of his life.

While God was having a meeting, satan came to His door. His visit didn't intimidate God; when you are great, your enemies never intimidate you. You don't read in the account about anybody jumping under the table in a panic and screaming, *'Oh Jesus! The blood of Jesus! Ooh, the devil! My God, hurry up! The devil is out there!'* It's funny how church people are always trying to get rid of the devil, but in that story God doesn't rebuke him; He doesn't bind him up, nor does He send him away. God invites him in and lets him sit down. Can you imagine satan knocking on God's door?

(Knock, knock, knock)

"We're in a meeting; who is it?"

"It's satan."

"Come on in satan; what have you been doing, boy?"

"I've been traveling to and fro through all the earth seeking whom I can devour."

"Oh you have, huh? So you've been on your job haven't you?"

"Yeah, I've been on my job."

"What do you think about my man, Job?"

"I never considered him; let me go check him out."

Satan went and sized Job up, then came back to God and said,

"Hold it, God; this isn't fair!"

"What do you mean?"

"You have a hedge around Job. I can't get to him. How do you know that he's all that you say he is if you have a hedge around him? He won't be able to prove you right because I can't even get to him to see what he is made out of. I'll bet you anything that if you move that hedge out of the way, I'll make Job curse you to your face."

"I'll tell you what; the next time you go down there, the hedge is going to be moved. You can have everything; you can touch everything, but don't touch his spirit; that belongs to Me. I guarantee that after you do all that you can do, Job is still going to worship, love and serve Me."

How awesome it is when God can brag on you like that; when He can testify about you and say, "Take your best shot! Whatever happens, my servant will worship Me!" It's one thing when you testify about yourself. You really aren't saying much when you tell it, but when God says it, what a testimony! Job went through everything! He lost his family; he lost his wealth; he lost his health; he lost all he had. He was lying in ashes with sores all over his body from the top of his head to the soles of his feet. Even his wife told him to curse God and die; yet despite his circumstances he never failed to worship and love God. Job says in the thirteenth chapter and fifteenth verse:

> *"Though He slay me, yet will I trust in Him: but I will maintain mine own ways before Him."*

While satan came to destroy Job, and stripped him down to nothing, he could not take away God's ultimate plan of prosperity for his life. Job survived satan's attack. He overcame the storm, and because of his faithfulness, God exalted him to a higher level of greatness in that He gave him *double* all he had lost.

Determine in your mind that you will be great, and that's it. Whatever you do and anything you accomplish will be great; it will not be something limited to a small corner. Although it may start there, when God gets finished with it, it's going to be so extensive, no one's going to be able to handle it!

Even if you are starting in, or have suddenly found yourself in a pit or basement, decide that it's not where you are going to stay and it's not where you're going to end. You may be starting in a hole, but you can end up on the mountaintop!

Go to a mirror and make this declaration to yourself:

"*I am coming out of this pit; I am coming out of this basement situation! I'm going somewhere because I serve a Great God! Greater is He that is in me, and because He is greater, I am greater. I look greater. I feel greater. I am greater. This is just the beginning! If you think I'm somebody now, hold on just a little while longer. You haven't seen anything yet!"*

From designing your blueprint, to preparing you as a builder, to laying your foundation and establishing your structure, God wants to reveal to you how you can build a Great House and achieve greatness in every area of your life.

✘ Building a Great House ✘

My Personal Construction Site - 1

✘ Have I been satisfied with mediocrity in my life?

_____

_____

_____

_____

✘ How can I improve my personal life?

_____

_____

_____

_____

✘ What do I need to do to improve my career?

_____

_____

_____

_____

✹ What would develop my family into greatness?

_____
_____
_____
_____

✹ Here is what I will do:

1) Acknowledge God in all of my ways and allow Him to direct my paths. *Proverbs 3:5-6*

2) _____

3) _____

4) _____

5) _____

✹ This is what I sense God has said to me through this chapter:

_____
_____
_____

Two

The Blueprint of a Great House

Every structure, before it's built, starts in the mind of an architect who has a vision of a magnificent edifice. Skillfully, he transfers the intricate details of what he envisions on to blueprint paper. He knows precisely the exact specifications, measurements and dimensions required to produce the design he intends. A person who is not trained to read a blueprint can't comprehend the complex details, fine lines, side markings, and abbreviations that, if followed, will produce the perfect and expected outcome. Their lack of understanding would cause them to look at the most glorious of plans and disregard them, thinking that it's just a bunch of senseless lines and figures on a sheet of messy paper!

God is not just any architect, but a Master Architect, and in the heart of God there is a blueprint for each of us waiting to be revealed which is hardly like the plans we have made for ourselves. Our plans many times are too limited and too small, and fail to meet the standards that God has purposed for us. God's plans for us are so much bigger than ours; He has great plans, not small plans for our lives. This is why it is important to seek Him and be willing to replace our plans with His. Don't allow the enemy to deter you with fear and intimidation, but rise up and dare to respond to God in faith, believing that by His blueprint your life will be better than anything you could ever dream. The Lord wants to expand your borders so that the life, career, or family you build will be a reflection of the great God you serve. Even if you are unable to understand the wonderful design God has carefully drawn out for your life, trust Him and be mindful not to dismiss His plan simply because you can't read or interpret the blueprint. Rest assured that God, the Master Architect, knows how to arrange and construct our lives so that the end result is greatness!

> *Be mindful not to dismiss God's plan simply because you can't read or interpret the blueprint.*

A Partner in the Building Project

> *"And, behold, I am with thee, and will keep thee in all places whither thou goest, and will bring thee again into this land; for I will not leave thee, until I have done that which I have spoken to thee of."*
>
> *Genesis 28:15*

In building your Great House, you will need the backing of a partner. A partner that will get in the trenches and work right along with you until the project is complete. God is that partner and He is committed to sticking with you through the entire building process and beyond. Not only does God give His word and His promise, but He also gives His support. He says, "Not only am I going to make you great, but I'm telling you that I'm going to work with you. I am going to back you up. I will make sure that you come into everything that I said you could have." We are workers together with Christ, because Christ is our partner. God has placed Himself in a partnership with us. Notice God said, "I am going to be with thee; I will keep thee in all places." It doesn't matter where you go when you're destined for greatness, because God, in His covenant with you, makes the commitment to stay with you until everything He has told you has come to pass. God stays with the project until you fulfill that which He has given you to do. That means, no matter where you go and no matter what the circumstances appear to be, if God is there, then He is going to ensure that your project doesn't go belly up; it won't go undone and incomplete. Even in negative circumstances, even in spite of your failures and your problems, and even in spite of your situation, God says, "I'm not going to leave you until I finish." With that kind of backing and support, you can move forward and onward, knowing that success is at the end of your journey.

> *In building your Great House, you will need the backing of a partner, and God has placed Himself in a partnership with you.*

Look at I Corinthians 3:9. This brings the principle in a little bit closer and helps us to understand some things about God.

"For we are laborers together with God: ye are God's husbandry, ye are God's building."

Understand that God is calling you to be a worker together with Him. The Word doesn't say *for* God, it says *with* God. That's awesome! Don't you know that if God is your partner in building something, it's done? If God is your partner, and is working with you, how can you lose? If God be for you, He is more than the world against you. It doesn't matter who is not on your side; it doesn't matter that people don't like you. It doesn't matter that others are talking about you. If God is on your side, you can't fail.

> *God is unwavering in His commitment to be with you and keep you until your Great House is completed, from beginning to end.*

Consider the place or the situation where you are today. Maybe it's not the best time in your life. Maybe you are looking out of the window of your life and it's cold, dark and rainy. You haven't seen daylight in months! You keep asking yourself if the sun will ever shine again. Be encouraged in knowing that God has not forsaken His intentions, but He's faithful to complete what He's started! God hasn't scrapped His plans regarding you just because of a rainstorm! He hasn't changed His mind because the sun went down! On the contrary, He's unwavering in His commitment to be with you and keep you until your Great House is completed, from beginning to end. This doesn't just apply to building a great church or spiritual life; it applies to building a great life as an individual, a great family, a great career or anything you plan to do.

�֍ Building a Great House ✖

Separation Through Relocation

> *"Now the Lord said unto Abram, get thee out of thy country, and from thy kindred, and from thy father's house, into a land that I will shew thee; And I will make thee a great nation."*
>
> *Genesis 12:1-2a*

When God told Abraham that He would make him great, He called him from out of his country and away from his kinsmen and the place of his familiarity, then placed him somewhere else. By faith, Abraham went on a journey to a land that he did not know; God relocated him so that He could reestablish him. Abraham could not become great until he left where he was and became separated from those things that would cause him to stay in the rut that he was in, and that would cause him to stay small and ineffective. Realize that not everyone wants you to be great. Some people want you to stay small and dried up, going nowhere, doing nothing and confined by circumstances and surroundings, just like they are. If you continue to live in the presence and under the influence of those people, guess what? You will never be able to develop beyond those conditions. You have to depart from the things that will keep you weak, average and mediocre. You have to move away from the negative influences that would otherwise hold you back. This separation is not limited to people and places, but it also includes the necessity to be separated from iniquity.

> *Depart from the things that will keep you weak, average and mediocre.*

You must understand that there is a difference between sin and iniquity. Sin is something that you do; iniquity is the thing that produces the sin. Now, great people make mistakes, but great people don't live in their mistakes. Great people make errors, but great people don't stay in their errors. In other words, even though you are great, the Word doesn't say you aren't going to make any mistakes; the Word doesn't say you aren't going to sin sometimes, but you are not to wallow and dwell in your sin. You are not to make a bed in it and become comfortable. You don't cover it and dress it up. You have to recognize iniquity and realize that it's not allowing you to go forward. Once you have come to that realization, you'll have to *sanctify*, or separate yourself from iniquity. The word sanctified does not indicate your style of dress, as some of us have been led to believe. The word sanctified means to be separated; to be sanctified means that God has separated you and has set you apart, that He might prepare you, or take you through a process that is going to make you ready for every good work. Paul says in II Timothy 2:21:

> *"He shall be a vessel unto honour, sanctified and meet for the Master's use, and prepared unto every good work."*

> *If you are going to be great, you will have to separate yourself so that you can be trained for the Master's use.*

If you are going to be great, you will have to separate yourself so that you can be trained for the Master's use.

When a person makes a covenant with The United States Government and agrees to defend our country in the Armed Forces, the very first thing that Uncle Sam does is sanctify him! He pulls that individual out of the place that he is familiar with. He doesn't set up boot camp in that person's back yard! No! He separates him from his home, his family, his friends, his state and sometimes his country! Have you ever seen someone go away for military training as a little boy or girl, but they return as a full-grown man or woman? How does that happen? Once that person has departed from all that is comfortable to him, from every luxury that he is accustomed to, and from any friend, family member or other influence that would hinder him, he is then able to begin a process of development. There is no one there to talk him out of or stop the development process, because he is set apart. There's no one there to pull him away from it because he is far outside of those inducing factors that would hold him back. When he returns several weeks, months or years later, some of his friends and buddies are still in the same place they were in when he left. They are still hanging on the same corners, playing the same games and running around in the same circles, content with mediocrity and accomplishing nothing. On the other hand, this man's life has changed because, during the time he was away he was being re-established, trained, and built up, for the Government's use!

The principle is the same. If you are ever going to be great, there are some things you are going to have to leave, and there are some people you will have to leave. There is a process that will sanctify you, build you up and prepare you for the Master's use. You can probably identify some of those things right now; things you know you need to pull back from; relationships you know you need to break, situations that you already know if you broke free of them it would cause you to elevate to the next level. Challenge yourself to list those things, then trust God to take you to a new level as you move away from them.

The Preparation Place and Process

Have you ever seen an area of land that was nothing but trees, then one day on your way home from work, you noticed the trees were being cut down, and the land was being cleared and leveled. Preparation was taking place for something to be developed on that land. The next thing you knew, a new subdivision of homes had been constructed. Before any great endeavor there is always a period of preparation. This period is not always an easy or comfortable one, but to the contrary, it's usually a painful, but necessary process. There are two factors you need to recognize and understand during this preparation period. The first factor is the place in which God raises you up; the second is the process He takes you through.

Before any great endeavor there is always a period of preparation.

Understand that God may prepare you in a negative environment, but during that entire period, He is working on you and preparing you for your Promised Land, your Great House. The land of your preparation is not the land where God is going to ultimately place you. He will raise and

�֍ Building a Great House ✖

prepare you in an Egypt environment. Egypt was a place of bondage for the Israelites, but just as God was building them up while they were there, He will build you up in Egypt. He will build you up in dark and strange places. He might build you up in a dysfunctional family, in poverty or in abuse. None of these places are easy to dwell in, but that place is your Egypt, the place of your raising, the place where you were neglected and the place of your suffering and pain. While you were in that place, people wanted nothing to do with you because they failed to see your true potential. That place is your Egypt, but guess what? God uses those places and circumstances to get you ready for a Great House in your Promised Land.

> *God may prepare you in a negative environment, but during that entire period, He is working on you and preparing you for your Promised Land.*

We see in Exodus 1:8-11 that Egypt's king recognized that the children of Israel were greater in number and in strength than the Egyptians to such a degree that he feared that one day they might rebel against them. To prevent this, he set up taskmasters to afflict them and make their lives miserable, but read what it says in verses twelve and fourteen:

> *"But the more they afflicted them, the more they multiplied and grew. And were grieved because of the children of Israel.*
> *And they made their lives bitter with hard bondage, in mortar, and in brick, and in all manner of service in the field: all their service, where in they made them serve, was with rigour."*

Now, although the Egyptians did all they could to keep the Israelites from growing and expanding, they could not contain them. You see, that is why you cannot get confused or depressed while you're in Egypt, because although the circumstances are not favorable, good things come out of Egypt. Ultimately, the hand of the king did not stop the Israelites from excelling and proceeding to Canaan, their Promised Land.

Knowing that, stop using your Egypt experiences as reasons for not going to your Canaan. Stop using your history as an excuse for your failures of the future. Stop using your past bondage as the reason why you can't enter into your Promised Land. Stop making excuses for your past, knowing that God was in your past, and God is in your present. God is going to be there when you get to where you are going. You might have been molested, but God says you are still a good thing. You may have been abused, but you're still a good thing. You may have been picked out and picked on, talked about, criticized and belittled, but know that what someone did to you cannot stop you from being who God called you to be. Tell yourself,

> *Know that God was in your past, and God is in your present. God is going to be there when you get to where you are going.*

"*I'm a good thing. Not only am I a good thing, I am going to become a great thing. I am not going to let my past or my Egypt experiences stop me from going to the next level.*"

✥ Building a Great House ✥

Just like the Israelites, when you come out of your Egypt, you will have experienced a great deliverance and you will have a great testimony!

Once you have been delivered from your Egypt, you must be prepared to go through the wilderness. The wilderness is your process; it's the place you have to go through to get to where you are ultimately going. While the Israelites had been freed from their bondage of slavery in Egypt, they did not enter into their Promised Land immediately; they arrived at the wilderness first. Although they weren't in Canaan yet, without delay they gave God praise; they sang songs exalting Him for their deliverance. There was a lady named Miriam, who, when she got to the other side of the Red Sea, broke out her tambourine and said, "If we are going to the next level, we have to learn how to praise God in the wilderness."

> *If you are going to the next level, you have to learn how to praise God in the wilderness.*

There is a lesson to be learned when we look at the children of Israel after they finished praising God for their deliverance. It wasn't long before they became discouraged and began to murmur and complain. They became thirsty and complained; they became hungry and complained. While they verbalized their displeasure to Moses, they were really complaining against God. Because of their complaining, immaturity and disobedience, they had an extended stay in the wilderness. Even so, God said to them *"Ye shall know that I am your God."* Some of you have rejoiced about being delivered from your Egypt, but have entered your wilderness perplexed and complaining. You will never get to where you are supposed to go with that attitude. You must continue to praise Him until you arrive at your destiny. Why? Because He has destined you to go to a great place. You are going to the place where giants live. You are going to a place where there is abundance, to a land of milk and honey, and you shall know that He is your God.

> *Don't allow the people and the circumstances of your Egypt and the process of your wilderness keep you from going into your Promised Land.*

Don't allow the people and the circumstances of your Egypt and the process of your wilderness keep you from going into your Promised Land. You've got to remember that even after deliverance came, Pharaoh chased after Moses and the Israelites with the intent of destroying them. The Pharaoh of your Egypt will try to chase, destroy and even drag you back to a place of bondage, but press on towards your greatness. The very ones who thought they were going to take your mind and your life, what are they going to say the next time they see you? When they see you happy and blessed, when they see you loving and praising God? What are they going to say? How shocked they will be when they were expecting an announcement of your funeral, and you send them an invitation to your mansion warming! Instead of coming to a burial, they'll be coming to a resurrection! What they thought was dead is yet alive. You know what? It is the thrill of my life, when I walk in the midst of people who just *knew* I was dead; I stand before them and say, "Behold; I live. You thought you killed me, but I'm only better, because I serve a great God!"

�֍ Building a Great House ✖

You have to understand that God did not make you to stay where you are, but He wants to bring you to another level. The God you serve doesn't want to leave you over in Egypt; God raised you in Egypt for greatness in Canaan. Though your Egypt may have been painful, God had a plan. Though you may be spending time in the wilderness, remember that God still has a plan, but the preparation period and the process is necessary in building a solid and stable structure that will bring glory to His Name.

My Personal Construction Site - 2

✖ What things do I need to separate myself from in order to achieve God's greatness?

_____
_____
_____
_____

✖ I have identified that these conditions hinder my progress:

_____   _____
_____   _____
_____   _____
_____   _____

✖ My personal Egypt experience:

_____
_____
_____
_____

✘ Building a Great House ✘

✘ My process to my Promised Land:

_____

_____

_____

_____

✘ I can see how God has developed me through:

_____

_____

_____

_____

✘ This is what I sense God has said to me through this chapter:

_____

_____

_____

Three

The Foundation

"The foundation of God standeth sure, having this seal, The Lord knoweth them that are His."

II Timothy 2:19

Any structure, in its entirety, can be no greater than the foundation, because it is the foundation that determines the height, the width and the depth of the structure. Whether you're building your personal life, your professional life, your family life, or your spiritual life, it must be built on a firm foundation.

The scripture shows us that God Himself understands that when you're going to build the foundation of anything, it has to be solid in order for the structure to stand. A Great House requires a solid foundation. When you don't take the proper time to make sure that your foundation is solidly built, then you will eventually get to a place where you can't go any further. Eventually you'll top out! You won't be able to go to the next level because you didn't start the foundation out right in the first place. The only house that is going to stand is a house that's built on the foundation of the Solid Rock. Paul says in I Corinthians 3:10-11:

> *"I am a wise master builder. I have laid the foundation and another builded thereon, but let every man take heed how he builded there upon, for the foundation can no man lay than that which is laid, which is Christ Jesus."*

> *If your house is built on the right foundation, you're going to persevere. You may have to go through tribulation, but you'll survive the storm!*

There are many structures being built, of which Jesus is not the foundation. He is not even the cornerstone! The foundation of everything we build has to be Christ Jesus. No other foundation you lay is going to be able to survive and stand through the storm it will inevitably go through. Even when you build right, storms are still going to come; trials will still come, but there is no need to be discouraged knowing that your foundation is sure.

Jesus tells the story in Matthew 7:24-27, of two men who each build a house. You know the story; one man built his house on sand, and the other built his house upon a solid rock. The one who built on the rock suffered the same trials and the same problems as the one who built on the sand. Both experienced the same rain, the same flood, and the same winds, but only one man's house stood. Why? Because the foundation on which that house was built upon was solid. If your house is built on the right foundation, you're going to persevere. You may have to go through tribulation, but you'll survive the storm!

The Bible says that God knows those that belong to Him. That means, when God knows you, and you know God, you are established on a firm foundation. Don't you know that when you really know God, and He really knows you, you cannot remain average? You have to expand. How far you expand depends on how excellently you've built the foundation of your relationship with Christ. The Bible says in Daniel 11:32 that we shall know our God, and because we know our God, we shall do exploits. Are you doing exploits or are you doing average stuff? Are you doing what everybody else is doing, living like everybody else is living, saying what everybody else is saying and just going along with the crowd, or are you doing some great things? I don't know about you, but I want to do exploits!

Inspection by Fire

> *"Now if any man buildeth upon this foundation, gold, silver, precious stone, wood, hay, stubble; every man's work shall be made manifest, for the day shall declare it and the fire shall try every man's work of what sort it is."*
>
> *I Corinthians 3:12-13*

When you are building a Great House, you can't just slap the foundation together out of any old thing. The material you are using must first go through a process. It has to be tried and proven to show that it is of the right quality, and sturdy and solid enough to build upon. It is the foundation that ensures the strength of the building, which is why you must take the time to perfect it. If you don't, no matter what you put on top of it, how much paint you use, or how you decorate the inside of your house, the entire structure will be shaky. We all know that pictures and decorations can enhance and beautify any home, but will those things stand in a storm? There will always be various items and furnishings in a building, some great, some small, some for honor and some for dishonor, but those things don't necessarily provide any type of stability. If you're going to have a great church, you can't have an unstable foundation. You can't have a group of people who really don't know about commitment, and going through the fire, and don't know how to deal with circumstances and consequences that are going to come against them. That kind of foundation won't stand. It has to be built a sure foundation. It has to be built in a way and in a means by which God gets the glory; the house that we build should be able to survive, because the foundation is right.

> *If we're going to build a great life, it has to be built on a sure foundation, and in a way by which God will get glory.*

While a house is being constructed, it must go through a series of inspections to declare its quality and safety. There are certain codes and requirements the foundation and frame must meet before further construction can continue. The inspector arrives with a thorough checklist and looks at many aspects of the unfinished house that a homebuyer would not even consider looking at or checking. He wants to make sure that the

✴ Building a Great House ✴

proper materials have been used to build the foundation. He looks for cracks, gaps and any signs that will reveal the structure's inability to stand, long before the walls go up and the carpet goes down.

There's a day coming before your Great House is completed that is going to test and determine what your foundation is built upon, what it is made of, and what you have built upon it. We've already established that it must be built on the Solid Rock of Christ. Now when we get to materials, the scripture first speaks of gold, silver and precious stones which are my preferences; how about you? Do you like gold, silver and precious stones or do you prefer costume jewelry and cubic zirconium? Then it speaks of wood, hay and stubble. Now of those materials, which do you believe would be able to survive a test fire? The Word says that every man's work shall be revealed by fire. What could that "fire" be? That fire could be

> *Don't be intimidated by the test; embrace it. When your house is built on the right foundation, the test is only going to prove it.*

opposition. That fire could be the trials and the things you are going to go through in order to bring something great into fruition. The fire is going to try every man's work to reveal exactly what it's made of. That means when you're building something and fire comes, there is no need to cry. There are many of us who say we want to be great, but when the fire comes, we're thrown into a frenzy. If we're building a house that will be a Great House which stands upon the right foundation of Jesus, when the test of fire comes, we're not going to panic. Don't be intimidated by the test; you ought to be able to embrace the test, because when your house is built on the right foundation, that test is only going to prove it. It will prove that testimony we gave; it will prove that what we said the Lord told us was really what the Lord said. Your work has to go through the fire.

Every item crafted of real gold that you have ever purchased could not be sold until it had gone through fire. The integrity of the metal had to be tested and proven. All impurities had to be burned out. The fact of the matter is, that gold, before it can be on your wrist, arm, neck, or wherever it is, before it shines and is valued at the price it is valued at, has to go through the fire. When gold goes through the fire, it gets better. When the fake stuff goes through the fire, it falls to pieces and disintegrates. Why? Because it is not real gold. Don't you know that there are many people who say they want to be great, but when it's time for the test of fire they either run or are disintegrated? Their whole world falls apart in the testing process. If, when you are tested, you can't take anything and you can't go through anything, it indicates that there are flaws in your structure. The fact that you are sensitive and the fact that everything hurts your feelings reveals that your work has some wood, some hay and some stubble in it. The test just comes to show you where you are. We ought to be glad about the fire because the fire just purges out all of the things that should not be there anyway. Sometimes when we lose things, we get upset because we thought that what we had was gold, but we found out that our works were crafted out of costume jewelry. If our works are of gold then that gold is

> *There are many people who say they want to be great, but when it's time for the test of fire they either run or are disintegrated.*

going to shine, while all of the other stuff will be destroyed. Guess what? We need that fire.

There is a test that will determine exactly what your character is made of. It will test your commitment; it will test your integrity. If you are lazy, it will be revealed by that test. If you don't know what it means to be faithful, it's going to show up on that inspection report. People who have built their houses, their lives, their organizations and their churches on the right foundation, don't worry or panic when the fire of trials come, because they understand that when the structure is made on and out of the right stuff, the results won't be disastrous, but instead their structure will be made better. If your foundation and its materials are made from the right substances, then God's glory is going to be manifested, because it will withstand the fire and pass inspection.

The Reward

> *"If any man's work abide which he hath built thereupon, he shall receive a reward. If any man's work shall be burned, he shall suffer loss: but he himself shall be saved; yet so as by fire."*
>
> *I Corinthians 3:14-15*

Here is something very critical that you need to know. If any man's work survives the proving fire, he shall receive a reward. A reward comes *after* we have gone through and passed the fire process. Are you expecting a reward without having gone through the fire? "Bless me with that car, Lord. Give me favor for that job I want. Fill up my bank account." We always want the rewards, but when it is time to go through the fire, we wimp out. The only *gifts* you receive are salvation, mercy and grace; those things God freely gives at no cost. If salvation had a price on it, guess what? The poor would die and the rich would live. If salvation were predicated on the works we did, most of us would not make it into heaven. I can tell you almost definitely that none of us would make it! Salvation is free, but as for the rest of it, you have to go through something to show yourself worthy of the reward. These other things we're believing God for, God doesn't just give those things to anybody. Rewards are not just given out. Rewards are for people who have come through and survived something.

> *Rewards are not just given out. Rewards are for people who have come through and survived something.*

Now every man whose work abides shall receive a reward, so if your work burns up, then what? You will lose your reward. If what you built does not survive the fire, you are going to suffer loss. But thank God for grace, because even if you don't become great, you can still be saved. You can at least make it through the Pearly Gates with smoke coming off the back of your britches, and with all of your stuff burned up, and say, "Lord, I just barely made it in here! Thank you, Jesus!" There are many who will do marvels and works and those works are going to burn up, but their spirits are still going to be saved.

Some people have the attitude of, "Well, I'm not worried about building anything. I don't want to do anything great; I just want to make it in." While you can and may make it into heaven, know that an attitude like that is not reflective of who God is, and will not help you to come into the destiny for your life that He has planned for you.

My Personal Construction Site - 3

⚒ I didn't realize it at the time, but my foundation and structure were being tested when:

⚒ The results of that test were:

⚒ I know now that the following impurities were burned away:

Building a Great House

✻ Did I pass inspection?

_____
_____
_____

✻ If I did not pass, why not?

_____
_____
_____

✻ When faced with those same circumstances again, I will make sure that I pass by:

_____
_____
_____

✻ This is what I sense God has said to me through this chapter:

_____
_____
_____

Four

The Materials of a Great House

"But in a Great House, there are not only vessels of gold and silver but also of wood and earth. Some to honor and some to dishonor."

I Timothy 2:20

Your Dream Home

How would you describe your dream home? The house that, when you look at it, takes your breath away because it is absolutely perfect and just what you have always wanted. What about its structure would you love the most? Maybe you're most attracted to its all-brick exterior; the bricks are the perfect color and texture, and bring uniqueness to the home like no other house in the neighborhood. As beautiful as those bricks are, don't you know that if the entire house were constructed with those bricks, it would be a structure most miserable?

You come to find out that not only is the exterior brick, but the entire interior is too! You can barely get into the house because the door is too heavy for you to swing open; after all, it's an all-brick door! Instead of having marble flooring in the foyer like you imagined, you discover that not just the foyer, but the entire floor throughout the house is made of brick. After only a short while, both your feet and all of your shoes would be entirely worn out from simply walking around the house. You can't park your car in the two-car garage, and you have to constantly wear a hard hat while you're in the house because you're afraid that the all-brick ceiling will come crashing down at any moment due to its weight! This is no dream house; it's a nightmare!

Perhaps you fell in love with a particular house because of its beautifully polished hardwood floors. Again, if the entire house were constructed of the wood used to make those floors, rather than it being a great house, it would eventually become a termite-infested, wretched house. Maybe your floors and ceilings would be okay, but the wooden bathtub and sink would drive you to bankruptcy because of the water damage that would occur. And what a disaster it would be to have polished and shiny hardwood toilets complete with hardwood sewer lines!

While there is nothing wrong with the brick or the wood, and both materials are good for something, as a matter of fact, they're great for something; neither is conducive for every purpose of the structure of a house. It takes all kinds of materials to build a great house; you can't just use bricks. You can't limit your materials list to one type of wood, or make the entire structure out of one material only. The house would not be able to properly function. If you're going to build a house that will stand

and operate the way it should, you have to understand that different materials will be used and are absolutely necessary.

> *If God is going to cause you to be great, you'll have to interact with people from all walks of life; not everyone will be like you.*

Just as there are all kinds of materials utilized in constructing a physical house, you as the builder of a Great House will have to deal with all kinds of people. If God is going to cause you to be great, you'll have to interact with people from all walks of life; not everyone will be like you. Not everyone will have the same economic base; not everyone will have the same family background or level of education, but if you're going to have a great house, you will need everybody.

Embracing Other People

There are many small, sanctified (yes, they are set apart!) churches that stand on one corner for years and never grow. The church is half-full with little, narrow-minded people there, who believe that they are the only ones who are going to see Jesus. They think that the only people in the world they can fellowship with are the members of their own little churches and congregations. They don't believe that they can rightfully fellowship with anyone else. They keep doing the same thing they have been doing for the last forty years and then make excuses for not growing. Do you know some of us are making excuses because we haven't grown? There are many Christians who are poor and broke, because they rejected the one whom God wanted to use to bless them and bring them out simply because that person did not look like them. Even people who do not believe like you believe, and lack a relationship with God have resources.

Do you recall in John 6:5-9 where Jesus fed the multitudes? Who was it that provided Him with the fish and the loaves of bread? It wasn't one of the twelve disciples; they immediately realized that they didn't have the resources to feed all of those people. It was a lad in the crowd who happened to have something that could be used. He had a resource that he surrendered to the hands of Jesus. Jesus utilized that resource to feed thousands.

You'll find another example of outside resource provision in Luke 22 for the preparation of the Last Supper.

> *"And he said unto them, Behold, when ye are entered into the city, there shall a man meet you, bearing a pitcher of water; follow him into the house where he entereth in. And ye shall say unto the goodman of the house, The Master saith unto thee, Where is the guestchamber, where I shall eat the Passover with my disciples? And he shall shew you a large upper room furnished: there make ready."*
>
> *Luke 22:10-12*

Again, the man who owned the house wasn't one of the twelve disciples, yet he provided the resource of an upper room.

One reason why some of us fail to achieve greatness is that we have limited our resources. We've gotten into a rut by confining ourselves to a small box of people. Realize that you can't restrict yourself to your own clique and clan and expect to grow. People who are going to be great realize that they have to interact with all kinds of people from all kinds of places, because they need them to become great. You don't have to be their best friend; you don't have to cut a covenant with them, but you have to have enough sense to know that people from all walks of life and cultures can help you. When you're connected to God's greatness, He will turn around and make even your enemies a resource provider for you. Even the ones who previously tried to stop you - God will arrest them and make them your friends for a season just to get you where you need to go. The ones who wanted to hurt you? The ones who thought they were killing you? He will arrest them and make them serve you for a season! As soon as you are committed to building God's house, He will build yours! When you are committed to building something great for Him, He is going to do something great for you; He is going to bring you out.

> *When you're connected to God's greatness, He will make even your enemies a resource provider for you.*

     Not only does II Timothy 2:19 mention gold, silver and wood, but it also says that there are things of earth in this great house. Now what is earth? Dirt. Don't you know that no house is a completely clean house? No matter how much you clean, there will always be some dirt in your house. The greater your house, the more dirt it is going to hold, but that doesn't mean that the house is not a great house. Some of us act like we have been saved all of our lives and we've never needed the mercy of God and the Blood of Jesus to wash us and cleanse us, yet the Bible states in Isaiah 64:6:

> *"But we are all as an unclean thing, and all our righteousness are as filthy rags..."*

Not just dirty, but *filthy* rags! Think about how you handle something that you consider to be filthy; you barely want to touch it! Well that is what our *righteousness* looks like to God, but just as God washed and cleansed us, He is yet drawing people into His house that will enter in dirty, just like you did. We as Christians have to be mature and stable enough to embrace them as they come. In some of our churches, we act as if there is no dirt there, and if we do realize some dirt, we try to ignore it. You have to know that in any house, there are always things that are in need of cleaning. Even if you are a "clean-a-holic" with an obsessive-compulsive disorder, walking around all day toting a bucket, wearing gloves and scrubbing everything you see, as much as you try, you can't get rid of all of the dirt. The reason why a person like that is classified as having a disorder is because the person continues to do the same thing over and over, and becomes frustrated and upset because they can't get rid of the dirt completely. You're *always* going to be cleaning in a Great House. The greater the house, the more you'll have to dust, mop, wax and polish. The greater the house, the bigger your vacuum cleaner has to be. The greater the house, the more cleaning supplies and products you'll need to keep that house halfway clean to the naked eye.

    Learn to embrace other people. How many precious and priceless treasures have been discovered because someone took the time to wash away a few layers of grime, or decided to make an investment in some tarnish remover? On the other hand, how many treasures have been tossed away as trash because someone failed to perceive the greatness and value of the item beneath the dust? The awesome thing about it is the item was priceless all the time! Don't limit and confine yourself to only utilizing one type of material to build your house; expand your borders. (Let me once again remind you that in order to do that, you have to have a *sure* foundation. If you are still trying to solidify your relationship with God, you definitely don't need anything or anyone to hinder you.) When your foundation is sure, you can deal with anybody. You can be all things to all people, make a positive impact on the lives of others, and benefit from the resources available to you.

My Personal Construction Site - 4

✗ Are my relationships with others limited to cliques?

_____

_____

_____

_____

✗ What can I learn from someone who is not like me?

_____	_____
_____	_____
_____	_____
_____	_____

✗ I can see where my growth has been restricted in the following areas:

_____	_____
_____	_____
_____	_____
_____	_____

✵ Building a Great House ✵

✵ These are the actions I will take to begin to embrace other people:

_____   _____

_____   _____

_____   _____

_____   _____

✵ This is what I sense God has said to me through this chapter:

_____

_____

_____

Five

Solomon Builds a Great House

> *"And behold, I propose to build an house unto the name of the Lord my God, as the Lord spake unto David my father, saying, 'Thy son, whom I will set upon your throne in thy room, he shall build an house unto My name.'"*
>
> I Kings 5:5

Solomon had the assignment of building God a Great House. He knew that he had to build something that was precious and beautiful. He also knew that he had to build it for God's glory. When God gives you something to build, you cannot build it small. In order for Solomon to produce something that would bring glory and honor to God, he had to have a plan. He realized that he could not simply hop out of bed one morning and expect to go outside and begin the construction of the house of the Lord. There are some key things that Solomon did which resulted in God's house being built.

Solomon Had Great Plans

> *"Then David gave to Solomon his son the pattern of the porch, and of the houses thereof, and of the treasuries thereof, and of the upper chambers thereof, and of the inner parlours thereof, and of the place of the mercy seat, And the pattern of all that he had by the spirit, of the courts of the house of the LORD, and of all the chambers round about, of the treasuries of the house of God, and of the treasuries of the dedicated things:"*
>
> II Chronicles 28:11-12

Even though King David himself was not allowed to build the house of the Lord because he was a man of bloody hands, God did give him the specific details by which this great house was to be built. David, knowing that Solomon would build the Lord's house, passed the pattern (or blueprint) on to him, so that this place of worship could be built as God instructed. If our lives are to be great, then we, like David, must get our pattern or blueprint from the Lord who made heaven and earth.

> *We must get our blueprint from the Lord who made heaven and earth.*

After you have received revelation of God's pattern for your life, you must develop a plan of execution to carry it out. A blueprint is practically worthless sitting on a table unused, even if you can visualize the finished structure. Until you begin to put some actions to it, it's just imagination. You need both a development plan and an execution plan. Too many times we leave the outcome of our lives to chance, and just wait for whatever is going to happen to us day-by-day. We fail to make and follow a plan that will take us where we need to go.

Have you ever seen someone who always talks about what they are going to accomplish *one day*? As the days pass by, they really aren't accomplishing very much at all. Why? Because they have no idea of what needs to be done to accomplish the goal that they have. They have failed to plan! They have a vision and blueprint for a Great House with no action plan! They don't know what materials are needed; they don't know of the resources that are available to them to help them. They don't have a timeline in mind. Instead of developing a plan of action, they just sit around waiting for the right roll of the dice to coincidentally happen. They wait for their number to come up. If that is not the case, then many times the plans the person does create are so limited and narrow that they still won't be able to construct what they may sincerely have in their heart to do.

There are people right now today who claim that they will be debt free, but fail to make a plan and a strategy to reach that goal. As the years go by, you hear them say things like:

"My debt is through in 2002."
"I'll be debt free in 2003."
"My debt's no more in 2004."
"Debt won't survive in 2005."

But guess what? Some of them are still in debt to this day, and will continue that way because they haven't planned a way out. They aren't fully aware of whom they owe; they don't know how much money to put towards the debts they have; they don't know which bills to pay off first! They may make a plan for three paychecks, and pay down half of one small bill, and that's the end of their plan! As a result, the great house they had in their mind to build never comes into fruition.

The plans you have may already be too small. Maybe you need to take your old plans and throw them away, then get yourself some bigger plans. God is saying to someone, "The plans you made are too small, because where I'm going to take you, you will have to have some great plans to get there." You have to get rid of your small visions. You have to get rid of your small dreams; you have to throw all of that matchbox stuff away. You have to see great things. You have to see yourself where other folks don't see you. You have to dream great dreams because you are never going to be any greater than your dreams. Develop a God-led action plan that will result in the completion of your Great House.

> *Develop a God-led action plan that will result in the completion of your Great House.*

Solomon Took Wisdom from a Mentor

> *"All this, said David, the LORD made me understand in writing by his hand upon me, even all the works of this pattern. And David said to Solomon his son, Be strong and of good courage, and do it: fear not, nor be dismayed: for the LORD God, even my God, will be with thee; he will not fail thee, nor forsake thee, until*

�֎ Building a Great House ✖

thou hast finished all the work for the service of the house of the LORD."

II Chronicles 28:19-20

Solomon had a great mentor in his father David who not only trained him to rule as his successor, but he also trained him in how to please God. David led his son in the ways of God through his own model and walk. Despite David's imperfections, he still kept a heart that was tender before God, and ultimately his desire was always to please God. David taught his son the fear of the Lord, causing him to understand the value of obedience and discipline in his life. Through his observation of his father, Solomon learned how to walk in the ways of God. Some people may not have the privilege of having a father (or mother) for a mentor, but there are many people around you that can mentor you and show you how to succeed at building your life into a great life.

You need to find somebody who is successfully doing what you want to do and interact with them. You ought to want a living example around you who can show you that God will not leave you where you are. You have to find somebody who can lift you up to the next level, not just in the church, but in anything you want to do. The key is surrounding yourself with people who will share with you the valuable lessons that they have learned, not only from their successes but also from their mistakes.

You will never be an eagle if you continue to hang around with chickens. If you stay in the constant fellowship of chickens, you will develop or continue the same habits and lifestyle of chickens. If you've been raised as a chicken, then that's all you're used to, and birds of a feather flock together. You will look like a chicken, peck like a chicken, eat, play, sleep, and act like a chicken! There may not even be anything wrong with being a chicken, but if you aspire to be great, and if you want to spread your eagle's wings, you can't do it in the barnyard! You have to stop hanging around certain people. Have you ever seen anybody come in the church, excited, and then two months later, that person is dead? That's because that person has hung around a bunch of buzzards. Buzzards just fly around, looking for dead stuff and stuff they can take advantage of. They're scavengers. An eagle doesn't want anything dead. Find an eagle. Again, you don't have to make a serious covenant, but get alongside that person and ask, "What did you do that brought you to the place where you are?" You may live in the projects, but nobody says you can't go visit uptown. Many people have started in the projects, but didn't stay there. You can find someone who has been able to get out of the projects and ask, "Now, how did you do it? I don't want to stay where I am too much longer. I want to go somewhere where there is abundance."

> *Surround yourself with people who will share with you the valuable lessons that they have learned, not only from their successes but also from their mistakes.*

Some of us have been in the same neighborhood for forty years; and because we've known our neighbor for twenty-four years and we have established a friendship with that neighbor, we have become comfortable. In all actuality, we've been in there twenty-three years, three hundred and sixty four days too long. Get out of there! Find somebody uptown and ask, "I don't want anything from you, but how did you get here? You haven't always lived up here. How were you able to rise above your circumstances and surroundings to get where you are today?" Some of us would rather stay where we are than get help. We'll sit there in our little houses and complain and get jealous of everyone else, when all we have to do is ask someone what they did. In doing so, God will see the intent of our hearts; God will see our faith and He can lead us to someone that will say, "Look here, I am going to show you how to go to the next level."

> *God will see your faith and lead you to someone that will say, "I am going to show you how to go to the next level."*

Every leader has to know that God wants him to be great so that his people can always pull from the resources that he has. How can a leader who is not going anywhere take the people following him anywhere? You ought to want the best for your leader because, through that, God is showing you that He can provide the best for you.

As pastors come and look to me for leadership, I can tell them about how I used to have to preach in one suit for two months. I'll be able to share with them of how I had to struggle from week to week and ride in a car with a torn-up roof. I had to climb in the passenger's door of my car to get to the driver's seat. I'll be able to tell them how I had to get to church by faith, having no gas in my car, praying all the way that the Lord would make everything all right. I can tell them how I had to preach in shoes with holes in them, to people who were sitting in dry-rotted pews with second-hand carpet beneath their feet. That's right! Then I can tell them that the God I serve, the *Great* God I serve did not leave me there, but He brought me out! He brought me out of the miry clay and placed my feet on a rock! Every time I think about it, I want to lift my hands and shout Hallelujah!

Solomon Utilized Outside Resources

"And Solomon sent to Hiram, saying:
'Now therefore command thou that they hew me cedar trees out of Lebanon; and my servants shall be with thy servants: and unto thee will I give hire for thy servants according to all that thou shalt appoint: for thou knowest that there is not among us any that can skill to hew timber like unto the Sidonians.'"

I Kings 5:2,6

As Solomon prepared to build God's house, he realized that what he needed he did not have, so he called on a young man named Hiram. This man Hiram was a heathen out of Sidon; he was not a saved man, but he was a skillful man. Although Hiram wasn't saved, Solomon, in his wisdom, incorporated this man into God's plan. Sometimes what you need is not in your house. Again, there are some people

> *Pray and ask God to show you the doors, the resources and the things that He wants to use to bring you out.*

who are not in your church and may not even be saved, who have resources that can help you go to the next level. You have to understand that when God gets ready to build a Great House, He is not limited to only utilizing the people you've been hanging around, but God just may direct you to people outside of your circle who have something that they can give you that will significantly help you. God will use anybody and He has proven that time and time again. God can even use a donkey to take you to the place where you are going. Don't despise the donkey; it may be an uncomfortable but temporary ride, so just ride him. Ride him until you get to the place that he's supposed to take you. If that is the thing God is going to use to bring you to the next level, then ride baby, ride!

We, as people of God, have to know that not everybody who is going to help us will be saved. Not everybody who will assist us will be in our little circle. They may not be saved, but they are still the resource that God wants to use when He builds His Great House. We have to expand ourselves and look beyond ourselves. The materials you need may not be where you are. Pray and ask God to show you the doors, the resources and the things that He wants to use to bring you out.

Solomon Requested Help from Many People

> *"Then King Solomon raised up a labor force out of all Israel; and the labor force was thirty thousand men."*
>
> *"Solomon had seventy thousand who carried burdens, and eighty thousand who quarried stone in the mountains, besides three thousand three hundred from the chiefs of Solomon's*

deputies, who supervised the people who labored in the work."

I Kings 5:13,15-16

Solomon employed the labor and assistance of thousands to accomplish the assignment given to him. He didn't try to do it alone and he didn't just get his best friends. He got help from more than one hundred and eighty thousand other men; don't you know it is the same thing with every aspect of your life? You need thousands of people. One or two of your friends cannot take you where you need to go; get yourself more friends, friends with a purpose. Of the people that Solomon employed, they all had a purpose which contributed to the end result. Some supervised, some carried materials, some cut stone, some cut trees. Expand your friendships to include more purpose-driven people who can help you!

My Personal Construction Site - 5

🛠 I have taken the time to hear from God concerning His plan for my life, and what He's shared with me is:

____

____

____

____

🛠 While I am believing the Holy Spirit to lead me, I have identified the following individuals who could mentor me:

Mentor	Area
____________________	____________________
____________________	____________________
____________________	____________________
____________________	____________________

🛠 What are my available outside resources?

____________________	____________________
____________________	____________________
____________________	____________________

🛠 What help do I need?

____

____

____

🛠 Do I have an effective action plan?

____

____

🛠 Here are immediate actions I will take to pursue my goal:

____________________ ____________________

____________________ ____________________

____________________ ____________________

____________________ ____________________

🛠 This is what I sense God has said to me through this chapter:

____

____

____

Six

Committed to Building the House

> *"Wherefore, holy brethren, partakers of the heavenly calling, consider the Apostle and High Priest of our profession, Christ Jesus; who was faithful to Him that appointed Him, as also Moses was faithful in all his house. For this man was counted worthy of more glory than Moses, inasmuch as He who hath builded the house hath more honour than the house. For every house is builded by some man; but he that built all things is God."*
>
> *Hebrews 3:1-4*

God shows us in His Word that faithfulness, one of the nine fruit of the Spirit, is a characteristic of any person who will achieve anything worthy of merit and glory. If you don't have an understanding of what it means to be faithful – not only faithful to God, but also faithful in anything you strive to accomplish – you will never become great. In

Hebrews, Paul says that Jesus was faithful to Him that appointed him, and Moses was faithful in his entire house. Moses was a man who brought glory and honor to God by fulfilling the will, the purpose and the plan of God. Moses was faithful in his service to God. Success is not going to automatically come to you simply because God is great, but we must understand that without faithfulness, we can do nothing great for God. There are some things you will have to consistently do in the area that you are striving for success in. If you want to become an awesome musician, guess what you are going to have to do? Practice faithfully. If you want to have a tremendous prayer life, you are going to have to consistently pray. Greatness is not achieved through osmosis or phenomenon. Some of us want to go to the next level, but we don't want to do what it takes to get there. There are many people who want to be great but they don't want to be faithful; they don't want to pay the price. The two don't match. There is a song that church folk sing all of the time, "Sometimes up, sometimes down, sometimes level to the ground;" you shouldn't live that song. You're never going to be great until you get some consistency in your life. You cannot waiver in your commitment. When you're not committed to greatness, God can't support you. When you sit there and you don't want to do what it takes to make your home, your office, your church, your family greater, then you yourself don't want to be great. You have just settled; then God's going to leave you right there by yourself. You can't

> *Greatness is not achieved through osmosis or phenomenon; without faithfulness, we can do nothing great for God.*

get in the kingdom of heaven and settle; if you really get God in you, and you get in God, you're not going to settle for bare minimum. People who have a genuine experience from the Lord and have a real relationship with God will never settle for average but they will be committed and unwavering to reaching their potential.

First a Servant

There is a common thread among all of the great people that God ever used; they were faithful servants first, and not just because they were lords over God's heritage. You have to understand that while building this great house, you have to be a faithful servant; people who become faithful servants are built into great houses. When you read about Moses, you find out that he is always referred to as God's servant. When you look at Joshua, he is always referred to as Moses' servant. Observe the relationship between Elijah and Elisha; Elisha served Elijah until he was caught up. And look at

> *He that is greatest among you, let him be as the younger; and he that is chief, as he that doth serve.*
> *Luke 22:26*

what Jesus says to his disciples when they contemplated amongst themselves who would be the greatest. He said let the greatest be as the younger, and he that is chief as he that serves (Luke 22:26). You have to understand this pattern that is shown to us in the Bible. Unfortunately, not everyone wants to take on the role of a servant. Not everyone wants to sit at the feet of another as part of the process of becoming great. A lot of people were in Israel, but don't you know only a few became great? There were millions of people in Israel, but only a few stood out. When you look at the ones who stood out, Joshua, Caleb, Aaron, all of them were faithful servants in another man's house. All of them served. Do you remember Aaron and Hur? While Israel was in battle, Moses was on the mountain interceding for them. He needed the support of Aaron and Hur to keep his hands lifted so that Israel could win the battle. What would have happened if Moses had not had these faithful servants in his company? Don't shun the role of a servant; if Moses hadn't had faithful servants around him, he would have never been great.

Joshua and the other men that served had to go through some things while serving Moses; there was a time when the people rose up against and wanted to stone Moses. Moses had three million people rising up against him, and only two or three people standing with him. In any kind of adversity, no matter what came or what the situation was, Joshua, Caleb, and a few others stood with the man of God. They said, "If you stone Moses, you will have to stone us." That takes some faithfulness. It takes some commitment to put your life on the line. Not everyone is willing to go down with you. (Remember the Titanic? When that ship started to sink, it was every man for himself. The passengers were trying to get off of that sinking ship the best way they could. Husbands were leaving their wives. Fathers were leaving their children. Wives were leaving their husbands and some were saying 'I hope he goes down with the ship!')

> *Sitting at the feet of another in servitude is part of the process of becoming great.*

There are a lot of churches that don't have the best leaders but every great church starts with a few people who believe in the God they serve, and believe that they have a great and holy man or woman of God leading them. Because they believe in the leader, they make the church great even when the leader is lacking. You see, every great church is supported by great people who have bought into the fact that the leader is a great man or woman of God. If they haven't, they will never see themselves, their leader, or their church come into a place of greatness. A great church takes great people who have built their lives on the proper foundation and understand their roles and their responsibilities, people who have been tried and proven to stand. If you're going to have a great church, you have to have some people who see great things, who believe great things and want to do great things. God is looking for people who will stop looking around for who is and isn't present, and start thanking Him for the greatness that is there already.

> *A great church takes great people who have built their lives on the proper foundation and understand their roles and their responsibilities,*

From Servant to Leader

We all recognize Moses as a great leader, and Moses spent a lot of his time building Joshua into a great man. After the death of Moses, Joshua was promoted to that leadership role. Do you think that Joshua always had fun while he was being groomed as a leader? His promotion did not come with ease but was a result of his commitment as a servant and student under Moses' tutelage. Joshua, who served Moses until his death, was honored by God because of his faithfulness and servitude. God said to Joshua, "Moses, my servant is dead, and because you have been faithful in Moses' house, I am going to magnify you in the eyes of the people." Moses was a faithful servant in God's house; Joshua was a faithful servant in Moses' house, and now God honored Joshua with the greatness, glory and honor that He had previously given to Moses. If you look into the lives of many elevated leaders; you will find that they not only sat at the feet of someone before them, but they diligently served that person. They stayed committed to that person. That doesn't mean that they always liked it, or their servitude was easy and enjoyable. None the less, many of them can share that they were in the perfect position to be groomed and developed for what they are doing today because they brought that person's coffee, they picked up the dry cleaning, they took notes, they ran errands, they typed letters, they served! They will tell you that they received key learnings in that servant role. After being faithful, paying the price and completing the process, they were promoted into their own leadership roles.

Encouragement For a New Leader

Even after you have been properly developed and trained, becoming a new leader can yet be intimidating. With a promotion comes a new level of responsibility with new hurdles to clear and new challenges to overcome. A new level of respect must be earned and maintained. After the death of Moses, God talks to Joshua because he needed some encouragement as a new leader. No longer did he have Moses to direct or guide him. He had to stand on his own, and rely on what he'd been taught along with his ability to seek God for himself. After you have been faithful in a house and you lose someone who has fathered you, who has developed you, and who has trained you to be what you need to be, the loss is tremendous. Any time you lose something great, it can have an adverse effect upon your life.   So when Moses leaves the scene, God reassures Joshua that He is going to do the same thing in his life; all of the training, all of the developing, everything that Moses did to build Joshua into a Great House, was going to pay off in his life. God not only honored Joshua; but He magnified him before the people. If you are a new leader today, allow God to encourage you, knowing that His promises are not limited to your predecessors.

> *With a promotion comes a new level of responsibility with new hurdles to clear and new challenges to overcome.*

Committed Beyond the Circumstances

When you are being built up and groomed for what it is that God has for you, you're going to have to make some painful sacrifices. You have to understand that if you're going to be what God wants you to be, you're going to go through some trials and situations. God can't develop you if you don't do some things that will take you through a process. Again, you can look at any great person, not just from the Bible, but also look throughout history at anyone who has done anything worthy of merit; that person's biography would reveal that that person has come through some awesome tests and trials. Those individuals are seen as survivors; they kept going when everyone else quit. That is not to say that they never stumbled, but they didn't quit. They pressed on when others said it couldn't be done. They persevered through accidents, rejections and devastating circumstances.

If you're going to succeed, you can't quit. If you're going to be what God wants you to be, you can't cry and give up every time something doesn't go your way, and every time something discouraging happens. Are you discouraged right now? Are you in a battle right now? If you are going to win, you have to stay until the end. You will tell the story, but God will get the glory. God is standing right there saying "Hang in there; you're going to make it." Don't quit. That is your word for today. Even if you're discouraged, don't quit. The minute you quit and are no longer encouraged to go on, you'll be incarcerated. The thing that makes you quit will keep you locked away, isolated and in bondage, never to be free. It looks like the closer you get to the thing that God wants you to have, the greater the enemy tries to attack and prevent you from obtaining it, but you have to hang in there. Even if it's all you can do to move your right foot only two inches in front of your left, it's progress. Faithfulness means that, in spite of what outside circumstances try to influence your life, you're already committed and set to do whatever it takes to go to the next level.

> *Faithfulness means that, in spite of what outside circumstances try to influence your life, you're already committed and set to do whatever it takes to go to the next level.*

God doesn't want any quitters; He needs some winners. It's not over until God says it's over. You have to stand up and say, "Lord, I'm here." That's what the seasoned saints meant when they said, "I came over here to stay, Lord!" They meant that the only way they would leave was by death. Because He that is greater is in you, you must be willing to fight to the death. Tell the enemy, "You can look at me funny and treat me any kind of way, but I'm not going anywhere. If you're going to get rid of me, you will have to kill me; I'll have to be dead. That means if there is one more breath in my body, and I cannot say a word, as long as I can lift my finger, I'm moving forward!" You will have to do as Jacob did when he wrestled with the angel and determine that you aren't letting go until you receive your blessing. You must be in it to stay! When you come out victorious on the other end, God's going to get the glory.

Carefully Constructed Pitfalls and Trials

God is the creator of all things; there is nothing you are going through that He has not built. Not only has God built your

> *God's not setting you up to fail; He's developing you to become great.*

blessings, but He's also built your test and trials. What I love about God is, if He built the test, He knows all the answers; He knows how to get you through what you are going through. He never puts you through anything in order for you to be defeated, and you ought to know that when you get out, you're going to be better. God's not setting you up to fail; He's developing you to become great. When you read about Joseph in Genesis, you find that God built a pit for Joseph. Potiphar's house and the jailhouse were also designed for Joseph, but God did not build those tests to destroy him; He built them so that Joseph could go to the top. That's why, when you get in a pit, even if you cannot see your way out, you have to be able to focus on God who made that pit. God does not design a pit for you to dwell in it forever. If He made the pit for you to get in, then He is going to make a way for you to get out.

> *God is the creator of all things; there is nothing you are going through that He has not built. Not only has God built your blessings, but He's also built your test and trials.*

If you're stuck in a pit, it just may be your attitude that's keeping you in there. You haven't realized who you are yet. If you don't realize who you are, you will be forced to stay there until you find out who you are. One day Joseph woke up; he came to realize who he was, and he found out that he didn't belong in the pit. He found out that the pit was not his home. His brothers may have put him there, but he was determined that he wouldn't be kept there. When you're great, people can put you in a pit but you'll come out. Joseph started making his way out of the pit, and you are going to have to do the same thing! Don't just sit there! If you are going to the next level, you have to shake yourself and start praising God and telling yourself, "I'm coming out of here." You have to get to dancing; you have to say, "I serve a great God, and I am not supposed to stay here for the rest of my life. I started here a long time ago, but it is time now for a change." You have to start coming in the house of God with praises in your mouth!

Building a Great House

Everywhere Joseph went, he prospered. He prospered in the pit; he prospered in Potiphar's house, and he continued to prosper. Not only did he prosper but everybody that was associated with him became better because he was there. You, right now, possess that same ability to prosper and affect those in your presence. Your family is going to be better because you're in it. Your place of employment is going to be better because you are there. Every place you go will improve. If your presence doesn't result in improvement, it's only because you haven't yet recognized who you are. When you go into a church, you should be able to say, "Glory to God, greatness is in this church because I showed up. This church may have some problems, but I am going to be an asset and not a liability. I came to bring something. This church is a better place because I'm here!"

> *Everywhere Joseph went, he prospered. You possess that same ability to prosper and affect those in your presence.*

Now while God has built all things, what the devil does is try to use what God has built to trip you up. You see, the same tree that God made to bless Adam and Eve was the same tree the devil used to defeat them. Be aware that the devil is going to try to use circumstances that God allows and has constructed for your life to cause you to fall.

Insight Beyond the Opposing Surroundings

In Numbers 13, twelve spies went into Canaan to scope out the Promised Land and found that it was indeed a great land, but it was also inhabited by giants. Twelve people went to the same place and saw the same thing and came back with different accounts, perceptions and opinions. Of the twelve surveyors, ten saw themselves as grasshoppers in comparison to the giants they saw. The ten spies who saw themselves as grasshoppers saw the same exact thing that the remaining two, Joshua and Caleb saw, but the way the ten saw it discouraged them and convinced them that they were not able to inhabit the land. But look at what Joshua and Caleb said when they got back. They said, "We are well able." They saw the same giants, the same challenges and the same potential barriers; however their perception of what they saw caused them to know that they weren't just able, but well able. What's important is not what you are going through, but the way you perceive what you are going through. If you perceive it right, you are going to come out right. Today, you are well able. When everyone else says you cannot do it, you have to say, "I am well able." The odds might be against you and the statistics may not be in your favor. You might be a single mother, but you have to know that you are well able. You might be on welfare, but you can say, "I don't care about welfare, because I am well able. I am going to come out of this situation. I am too great to stay here." It's not your situation that's hurting you; it's the way you are looking at it. You have to change your perception and stop seeing yourself as a grasshopper. When you see what God sees, you will have a totally different perspective.

God met Joshua right before he went into Canaan and said, "This day, I am going to magnify you." If God doesn't magnify us, we are

> *When everyone else says you cannot do it, you have to say, "I am well able."*

nothing. We are grasshoppers unless God magnifies us because we can do nothing without God, but when God magnifies you, even the giants look small. When God magnifies your mind, you're going to see things differently. The Bible did not say that the giants shrunk, but Joshua said, "The Lord has magnified me." In other words, God is going to make you bigger than your problem. He's going to make you greater than what you're going through. You need to let the God you serve expand your mind and expand your vision; then instead of seeing yourself as a grasshopper, you will see that problem as a grasshopper! It used to look like a giant, but because the Lord has magnified you, that same situation looks like its name is Tiny Tim. You aren't worried about Tiny

> *When Christ is formed in you, you won't be intimidated by your situations and your problems.*

Tim when the Lord has expanded you. You can turn cancer into Tiny Tim. You can turn poverty into Tiny Tim. It's not your problem that is going to change; it is you that will change. The problem is not getting any smaller; you just have to get bigger—bigger dreams, bigger visions, a bigger mind, a bigger spirit—until Christ is formed. Some of you have the little baby Jesus living inside of you. Jesus as a baby was just that, a baby. Babies are defenseless and helpless. Yes, even Baby Jesus. If that were not so, his earthly parents would not have had to leave the place of his birth to flee from King Herod who sought to destroy Him. The baby Jesus could not fend for Himself, but the Bible says He waxed strong; He developed; He matured into Christ Jesus. As Christ Jesus, he healed the sick, raised the dead and cast out devils! When Christ is formed in you,

you won't be intimidated by your situations and your problems. You won't back down. You won't give up.

The only reason that the situation is getting the best of you is because you don't know that the Lord has magnified you. While you are praising Him and going through, you have to see the situation shrinking. When God says He is going to magnify you before people and before your enemies, then the devil, who is a giant, has no more power over you. You will look that devil in his face and say, "You're going down tonight, with your little, tiny, short self."

> *"Lord magnify me so that I can glorify you. If I am magnified, You will be glorified."*

When God sends any great person into any desolate or challenging place, He never sends him or her there to fail. He always sends His people to conquer. The reason He sent you into that place was not because the place was great, but because you were. When you're magnified, He's glorified. When you go to work tomorrow with this anointing on you, people will ask, "What happened to you? It looks like you've been magnified." You're not going to die. You're not going to give up. You're not going to quit. You're just going to let the Lord magnify you. Right where you are, lift your hands and tell God, "Magnify me, Lord, so that I can glorify you. If I am magnified, You will be glorified."

✘ Building a Great House ✘

An Attitude of Worship

There is a common characteristic present in people who don't really know that God lives in them. They live defeated, destroyed lives, because they are always looking for motivation and answers from others, and then they get frustrated and more discouraged when no one can give them what they are looking for. When God calls you to a place and connects you to a purpose, He does not always give you outside motivation. Do you know why they can't find the answers? Because they are seeking in the wrong places, and all the while the answers are already on the inside. The Bible says the Holy Spirit will lead you and guide you to all truths. He will be your comforter. He will be your friend. He will be the one to show you God's ways.

When we don't realize how great God is when He chooses us, we will complain about petty issues, and let little things rob us of big blessings. We are too busy worrying about our problems rather than honoring the God who chose us. Let

> *When God calls you to a place and connects you to a purpose, He does not always give you outside motivation. We have to believe God, who dwells on the inside of us, more than we believe the world on the outside.*

me ask you something; if you really knew who was living inside of you, would you continue to act the way you've been acting? Would you deal with situations like you're currently dealing with them? Would you say the same things out of your mouth that you're saying right now if you really recognized the great God living inside of you? Would the words "I can't" come out of your mouth again? Would the words, "what are we going to do?" escape from your lips? Would you whine and cry and say, "I guess I'll never be what God wants me to be?" Would that ever come out of your mouth again if you really knew who was living on the inside? You can do all things!

When you become God's house, the only right you have is to worship. Anything that comes out of your mouth that is not worship discredits the God who lives inside of you. You have the Master of all creation living inside of you saying, "I am with you. I will expand you. I will make you great, and I won't leave you until everything I have said about your life comes to pass." I have to ask myself this question: how can I ever go into God's presence with an attitude again? How can I ever go into God's presence complaining and accusing him of failing me? How can I ever go to God, even in the roughest situations in my life, and tell God that He did not live up to His end of the bargain, when all the time God is saying, "I live here! Why don't you let Me be God? Why don't you acknowledge who I am in you, and let me deal with the problems you face for a change?" What more can we ask for? What we have to do is believe God, who dwells on the inside of us, more than we believe the world on the outside. Change your words of complaint into words of worship.

The Product of Commitment

Know that the end result of your faithfulness and commitment is excellence. Many of you who are reading this book are wonderfully gifted and talented. There are singers, musicians, artists, writers, computer

� Building a Great House ✠

wizards, athletes, etc. How many of you were born with those talents perfected in you? I mean straight from your mother's womb, you were at your absolute best. None of us have that testimony. As strong as that gift or talent may be today, it had to be developed and perfected, but it would have never developed had you not worked on it and practiced, pressed and persevered. You had to remain committed to its development.

> *The end result of your faithfulness and commitment is excellence.*

Some of the world's greatest musicians, as children, spent hours upon hours practicing, and hated it! And have you ever seen a depiction of an author ripping countless sheets of paper from a typewriter, balling them up and starting over, in an effort to write a best seller? And what about an athlete who presses on after sustaining what was determined to be a career ending injury? Surely they all faced adversity and challenges, opposition and trials, but had they given up, where would they be today? Know that in the pursuit of your greatness, you are not always going to feel like moving forward. You're not always going to feel like serving. You might have some seasons where you just want to throw in the towel. But even when you are weary and feel broken, you always have to have the attitude of, "I'm tired, but I haven't gotten there yet. I have to press on to the next level. This is not where I am supposed to be. No; I have to go beyond this. I'm striving for something greater. I'm not staying here in this mess. I'm in a zone now where I'm leaving everything that's weak and pitiful and I'm leaving everybody who wants to play games; I can't hang around here any longer." People will look at your undying diligence against the odds and say, "You're crazy. What's wrong with you?" You should tell them, "No, I'm not crazy; I have something on my mind. God is taking me somewhere. I have to be great. If I stay here with you, I'm never going to be anything, but I feel God calling me to another level. God is bringing me up and out. I don't have time to play with you."

> *Our attitudes, our spirits, the way we walk, what we accomplish, everything we do, we have to do it with a press and commitment of excellence because God is excellent.*

Our attitudes, our spirits, the way we walk, what we accomplish, everything we do, we have to do it with a press and commitment of excellence because God is excellent.

✘ Building a Great House ✘

My Personal Construction Site - 6

✘ My level of commitment can be best described by saying:

_____
_____
_____
_____

✘ I currently serve others in the following areas:

I Serve	Through
_____	_____
_____	_____
_____	_____
_____	_____

✘ In serving and/or as a leader I've faced these challenges:

_____	_____
_____	_____
_____	_____
_____	_____

✘ The pitfalls that tested my commitment were:

_____   _____

_____   _____

✘ Through these challenges, what caused me to stay committed was:

_____

_____

_____

✘ My perception and insight causes me to see these situations like so:

The Situation	My Perception
_____	_____
_____	_____
_____	_____

✘ This is what I sense God has said to me through this chapter:

_____

_____

_____

Seven

Reflecting God's Glory

"For I am the LORD that bringeth you up out of the land of Egypt, to be your God: ye shall therefore be holy, for I am holy."

Leviticus 11:45

A Reflection of Who God Is

A home builder many times will create a specific feature in the construction of a home bearing his name, as a trademark of his work, to make the home distinct and recognizable. One builder might always feature living rooms with vaulted ceilings. No matter the model, layout, or design of the home, if it has been constructed by that particular builder, the living room will feature vaulted ceilings. This distinction makes it easy for any other builder to immediately recognize his work because the design is a reflection of the builder. That builder wants his name to be associated with his work of distinction, and his excellence and quality of craftsmanship.

Likewise, in the spirit, anything God makes must reflect who He is. When God created you, He did not create you to be an insignificant, beat-up, crying and whining Christian. He created you for much more than that. He presents himself as an example of what He wants you to be, even through your adversity and calamity, and the place of your Egypt. Remember, we defined Egypt as the uncomfortable and painful place of your upbringing. Again, we know that it was difficult being raised there. You experienced suffering, hurt, rejection and circumstances that had the potential to destroy you. But God has brought you out of Egypt and commands you to be holy, for He is holy. He saw what you went through and He's brought you out. He saw what you were up against and He's delivered you. Now God, knowing the wounds that have inflicted you, also knows that it's not over for you. Even through all you have suffered, He knows there is yet excellency to be reflected from your life. You serve a God who stands as your example to be excellent.

> *Even through all you have suffered, God knows there is yet excellency to be reflected from your life.*

Some people say, "I know Jesus" and the world looks at them and asks, "You know *who*? You're full of issues; you're always pitiful; you can't seem to get yourself together, but you call on the name of Jesus? You look like you serve an old, dead, dried-up God." I can imagine God in heaven saying, "Did you say you're in a relationship with Me? Don't tell anybody else; keep that to yourself. Don't tell anyone else you belong to Me, because whatever I make, I want it to reflect who I am."

Whatever God does, He's going to bring glory to Himself. You see, God's not going to do anything little, and He's not going to make anything insignificant. He's not going to make anything that will fail. If He made you, then it automatically means He made you to succeed. He made you to go to the top. He made you to be as great as you can be and He won't settle for anything less because it would not properly reflect who He is. He made Adam in His own likeness and in His own image; that's why Adam was an awesome creation, fearfully and wonderfully made, patterned after and sculpted by the very hand of God.

> *I will praise thee; for I am fearfully and wonderfully made; marvelous are thy works; and that my soul knoweth right well.*
> *Psalms 13:14*

You have to understand that some of us have a lot of adjusting to do in our minds, the way we think, the way we act, the way we talk and the way we walk. It's sad to say, but many people, rather than having a mentality of excellence, have a defeated mentality and a mentality of wanting to get over. Some of us are conniving and always trying to come up with a plan or a scheme to get by. The Bible didn't say that we're supposed to be 'get-overs;' it said we are to be *overcomers*. If you're going to be an overcomer, you will have to get rid of that manipulative, get-over, wanting-something-for-nothing spirit. You can't manipulate yourself to greatness; you can't get there by using tricks and playing games. Don't just try to get over; overcome!

Jacob was that way, full of tricks and games. We all are familiar with how he manipulated his brother Esau and deceived his father Isaac so that he could get the benefits of a birthright that did not belong to him. As a result, he had to flee for his life! What is excellent about that? Now when God got a hold of Jacob, He said, "As long as you are a slickster and a trickster, I can't use you; you don't reflect My glory." So what did God do to Jacob? He separated him unto Himself on a mountain called Bethel, and He began to deal with him. He said "Your name is Jacob, which doesn't represent Me, and as long as your name means 'get-over' you can never represent Me; however when I get finished with you, you are going to be an overcomer. In order to reflect the fact that you are an overcomer, I have to change your name from Jacob to Israel. That name reflects who I am; it reflects the fact that I am the Father over my sheep. It reflects My glory." See, sometimes, in order for God to change you and your name so that you will become a representation of who He is, He has to wrestle with you. When that angel, sent by God, got a hold of Jacob, and Jacob got a hold of that angel, they turned each other every which way but loose. In the end, not only did Jacob get up a great man, but he had a great name.

A Great Name

What impact does a great name have? Some names you hear excite you, while others make you disgusted. Some names you hear embarrass you, and others make you feel proud. Just to hear some names make you exclaim, "Oh Lord," because you know what that name represents. All of us know of at least one person who can step into a negative situation and

Building a Great House

turn that situation around, because he is great, and we get excited when we hear that person's name. And in the same fashion we know how we feel when we hear the name of a person who is known for making a mess or starting trouble. Think about what comes to mind when you hear these names:

Timothy McVey *Former President Ronald Reagan*
Judas Iscariot *Osama bin Laden*
Martin Luther King Jr. *Sadaam Hussein*
Jeffrey Dahmer *Michael Jackson*
Tiger Woods *Abraham Lincoln*

What do those names represent in your mind? Now what does your name represent? What comes to people's minds when they see or hear your name? You have to want your name to be great. When you get connected with the Name that is above every name, when you get connected to Jesus, you can't stay small. You have to become great.

> *What comes to people's minds when they see or hear your name?*

Some people have the attitude of "I don't want anyone to know who I am; it's just little old me," but that has never been God's attitude towards who you are. He said to Abram, "I am going to make you a great nation. I will bless thee, and I will make your name great." God needed somebody in the earth to display His greatness to everyone else. He wanted somebody who was doing more than just singing 'How Great Thou Art!' He wanted others to know that Abraham served a great God. God made it so that every time people heard his name, they would think about Jehovah-Jireh. Every time they heard 'Abraham,' they would think about God and know of His awesome and mighty power. How would people know that there is a great God if He can't find great people, with great names that give Him glory? God is saying, "I want to make you a great nation and I want your name to be great." Allow God to change your name into a great name.

> *What you're doing should have a powerful and unique effect on something or someone.*

Manifesting His Glory

Every person whom God has ever cut a covenant with, went on to do something and build something great that represented the perfect nature of God. Everything those people did earned a monumental place in history, and the things that were accomplished by the individuals who were in right covenant with God, we are still talking about today. Why? Because when God builds something, He gives it glory. When He gives it glory, the creation knows that it did not bring glory to itself, but it has the glory that God gave it. Realize that you can never bring glory to God unless you are producing something great. Something has to be birthed; you have to manifest something; something tangible has to be seen in your life. What you're doing should have a powerful and unique effect on something or someone. You have no business doing anything halfway, just thrown together, and done just so you could get by. Everything you do should reflect the awesomeness of God.

�֍ Building a Great House �֍

Some people think they bring glory to God by the way they sing. Some people think they bring glory to God by coming to church. If you're coming to church and you're not building anything, not doing anything, not making things happen, not shaking, rattling and rolling, if you're not accomplishing great things, then how is God going to get the glory? You're just a sounding brass and a tinkling cymbal. You have to do something. If you don't, then you really can't bring God glory. How much glory is God getting out of your life if you are not building anything for him to get glory out of? I don't want to hurt anyone's feelings, but we have to understand that simply saying "Glory to God!" does not give Him glory. Saying "Glory to God" is good, but if you are not building anything, you are just saying something. "Glory to God! Hallelujah! Thank you Jesus! Lord you are an awesome wonder!" That sounds good doesn't it? But Jesus brought glory to God because He manifested God's glory. He brought glory to God through the manifestation of something that he built. When he conquered death, hell, and the grave, when He came down and built those disciples and made them great disciples and apostles of the church, then He built something that God received glory out of. Remember that the One who built the house always gets more honor than the house that was built. Although God gives the thing He's built glory, He Himself is glorified. When God glorifies you, He glorifies Himself. When he makes your name great, His name is made greater. When people see you and how awesome you are, they have to know that the God you serve is even more

> *When people see you and how awesome you are, they have to know that the God you serve is even more awesome!*

awesome! People have to know that when they are looking at your image, they are only looking at a symbol, a partial piece of the Creator. It is only when men see the manifestation of your works, that God gets glory.

Look at how Jesus reflected the glory of God. Jesus was famous; the Bible says, because of the great deeds He did, His fame spread abroad. He was famous but He gave God all the credit and the glory for everything He did. He said, *"I can do nothing of myself. The Son can do nothing without the Father."* Even Jesus, the Son of God, made sure that whenever people tried to give Him credit, He gave it right to God. There is nothing wrong with somebody giving you something when you give it to God. Now, if you are going to try to keep all the glory to yourself and act like you are responsible for it all, then you're going to get in trouble. When people shove glory to you, you should give it right back to God. When you give God glory for what He's done, He'll always do things through you, because you have shown Him that you know where the glory belongs. When you know where the glory belongs, God doesn't mind letting you have some of it. Some people say "I don't want anybody to see me!" Well, if you are the image of God manifested in the earth, how are they going to see God if they can't see you? How are they going to see what Jesus is doing if they can't see you? God doesn't mind it when someone tells you, "Ooh, you did a fine job!" Christians think they are supposed to respond by saying, "That wasn't me; that was Jesus." Oh,

> *When you give God glory for what He's done, He'll always do things through you, because you have shown Him that you know where the glory belongs.*

come on, that is false humility! That was you! But who gets the glory? God does. The natural man cannot see God and the fullness of His glory, but man can see you, and you're supposed to represent God. So when natural men see you acting like God, talking like God, doing things like God, then God says, "Alright! You are representing Me well. You're doing a good job. That's giving Me glory." In other words, you make God look good; God's happy about you. God's not happy about Christians who are just walking around sad and dejected, talking about each other, running their mouths and criticizing other people. God doesn't get any glory out of that. You can only reflect God's glory when you're moving forward and doing great things.

> *The Holy Spirit comes into your life to help you reach your potential, come into your destiny, and achieve the greatness that God has planned for you.*

The Assistance of the Holy Spirit

Do you know that the Holy Spirit comes into your life to help you reach your potential, come into your destiny, and achieve the greatness that God has planned for you? There are many Christians who aren't living great lives, but are living dreadful lives instead. Do you know when you don't live your life to your full potential, when you don't come into the greatness that the Holy Spirit inside of you had destined for you, you're grieving Him? What do I mean by grieving the Holy Spirit? I'm not talking about smoking dope. I'm not talking about committing adultery. A sin situation is not the only time the Holy Spirit is grieved. Yes, He is grieved when we sin, but He is also grieved when we sit there day after day with a loser attitude, when we sit there with an "I can't do it" attitude, when we sit there, saying, "Well nobody loves me and I will never do it. Woe is me." What you don't understand is that the Holy Spirit is in you to make something out of your life. He's there to take you to the next level. The problem is that the religious church has told us that if we don't smoke, and if we don't drink, then we are not grieving the Holy Spirit; yet every day that you sit there and act like you don't know who you are; the Holy Spirit is grieved. You have the power of God through the Holy Spirit dwelling inside of you, and you have Him all balled up; He can't go anywhere, or do what the Father told Him to do, because He's living inside of someone who feels like a failure. At the same time, I can imagine the Holy Spirit saying, "Lord, why did you put me in here?" The Holy Spirit doesn't want to see you sit there and waste your life crying at your own pity party. When the Holy Ghost comes into your life, He doesn't come in to make you a halfway Christian. He doesn't come in your life so that you can just barely get by. No; He comes so that you can fulfill your destiny. God has had great plans for you before the foundation of the world. Didn't the Lord say, "I will be with you?" Didn't He say, "I will go with you?" Didn't He say, "I will stand with you?" Then what is the problem? The Bible says in Daniel 11:32:

> *God has had great plans for you before the foundation of the world.*

�֍ Building a Great House �֍

"But the people that do know their God shall be strong and do exploits."

The God of the universe lives on the inside of you. This God creates galaxies! This God creates worlds! He speaks to the sun and the sun gives light! He speaks to dead things and they get up! The God you serve is used to opening up Red Seas. He is used to doing mighty things. Now, can you picture a great big God sitting in some person who's living a defeated life? Understand what I'm saying. You have stopped smoking and drinking; you're attending church faithfully and you love the Lord, but your life isn't going anywhere. You're no better off than you were last year. Can you see the frustration of God sitting in people who don't believe in themselves? The Holy Ghost in you knows that you're great; you simply haven't found out yet. The Holy Ghost can be living in your house and in your mind, and you might not even recognize that He is there. That's what Jacob found out. He said, "Lord, you have been here, and I didn't even know it." People say they have the Holy Ghost, but after they've received Him, what has happened? They may speak in tongues, but after they've spoken, what are they doing? Is there a manifestation of His presence in their house? You are the temple of God, and the spirit of God dwells within you. He is not just visiting, He dwells. He abides. He inhabits and lives in your house. If you have the Holy Ghost dwelling in you, you should be able to explain what He is doing with you. You have the

> *You are the temple of God, and the spirit of God dwells within you. He is not just visiting; He inhabits and lives in your house.*

creative power of the universe living inside of you, and He doesn't want to spend seventy to eighty years inside of you just to do nothing, just for you to barely get by, and all He can say is, "I came." He comes inside of you because He wants you to take on His attributes. He wants you to take on His nature. He wants you to be a creative force. He wants you to be able to create something where there is nothing. God is looking for somebody that will go where no man has gone before and do something that nobody has done before.

    Declare that next year this time, you are going to be greater than you are right now. Declare that your family will be greater; your finances will be greater and everything that God has given you will be bigger and better. There should be enough greatness built up in you right now just by you reading this book to turn your life and your whole city upside down. The Holy Spirit came to make you wonderful and make you great so that your light could shine and man could see your great works and glorify the Father in heaven.

✹ Building a Great House ✹

My Personal Construction Site - 7

✹ God's glory is reflected through me when I:

_____

_____

_____

_____

✹ When people hear my name, they think:

_____	_____
_____	_____
_____	_____
_____	

✹ What about those perceptions need to be changed because they don't reflect God's glory?

_____

_____

_____

✘ I have grieved the Holy Spirit by:

_____

_____

_____

_____

✘ I need the assistance of the Holy Spirit to help me reach my potential in these areas:

_____   _____

_____   _____

_____   _____

_____   _____

✘ This is what I sense God has said to me through this chapter:

_____

_____

_____

Eight

Recognizing God's Presence

"And Jacob awaked out of his sleep, and he said, surely the Lord is in this place; and I knew it not. And he was afraid, and said, how dreadful is this place!"

Genesis 28:16-17a

Do you know how many people come to church looking for the blessings of God because they don't realize that the Lord is in them before they even get there? Surely the Lord is in that place, and they don't know it. There are people singing about the Lord, there are people preaching about the Lord, and they know about Him, but they don't know Him. It's one thing to have a testimony about God, but it's another thing to know the God of your testimony. It is one thing to know that the Lord brought you out, but it's another thing to know the Lord that brought you out. Don't you know the Israelites knew that the Lord brought them out of Egypt, but they didn't have a personal relationship with Him? They knew about Him, but they didn't know Him. It's possible for you to have a testimony about God's deliverance in your life and not even know the Lord that delivered you. It's possible to sing about the Lord, and how good He is, and not even know the Lord you're singing about. Jacob came to the conclusion, *"The Lord was in this place and I knew it not."* Sadly, that is the testimony of many churchgoers. For some of us, the Lord has come right into our lives, saved and delivered us from our sins, and has come into us and made us His habitation and we've not even recognized Him.

> *If you don't know that the Lord is in your house, you'll disregard and misunderstand Him.*

After Jacob realized that the Lord had been there, he became afraid. Now, how can the Lord be in your house and it causes you to be afraid? Jacob's fear came from not having a right relationship with the Lord. It's one thing for the Lord to be in your house, but it's another thing for you to recognize His presence. If you don't know that the Lord is in your house, you'll disregard and misunderstand Him. You won't be able to enter into a right relationship with Him.

How can we have the Lord walking around in our house and not have a relationship with Him? In the same way that some of us have spouses at home, but don't have right relationships with them. Just because they are in your house doesn't mean that the relationship is solid or intimate. You can be living right in the house with somebody and not even know who that person really is. You can be tied to a person in name and legalities, but when it comes to covenant, there is none. There are men right now, who have been married for twenty years and because of the lack of proper relationship, are afraid to go to sleep at night. They sleep guarded, with one eye closed and the other opened because they don't know whom they are living with. Anytime you are attempting to sleep in a house with a woman, and you don't know if or when she might try to throw boiling water on you, you are scared! Waking up under a blanket of hot grits or with your bed on fire would be awful! There are couples that are living together, but the man is afraid to go to work for fear that when he gets home the furniture will be gone! "Why did you leave me, Lucille?" This is what happened: that man didn't really know Lucille. He was minding his business and the next thing he knew, Lucille was gone! People make statements like this: "I never saw it coming;" they were living with people whom they did not know.

When God found Jacob, Jacob had no real understanding of who God was. Jacob was not looking for God; God was looking for Jacob. Jacob didn't really care about God; Jacob was lying there, minding his own business. He wasn't having a prayer meeting. He wasn't 'seeking.' When the Bible says he was 'tarrying,' it means he was going to lie there all night and catch some Zs. He wasn't chanting and waiting for the Lord to fill him. He wasn't thinking about the Holy God; he was trying to figure out how he was going to get away from Esau. While he was snoring, not even thinking about God, God visits him and says, "Wake up. I'm going to give you some dreams. I am going to let you see Me for who I am, because I don't see you as Jacob; I see you as my tabernacle. I see you as Israel. I see you as a great nation." Later, when Jacob realized that God had visited him, it scared him to death. Jacob said, "The Lord was here all the time, and I didn't even know it."

Now, don't look down on Jacob. If you are honest with yourself, you will have to admit that when God came to see about you, you weren't thinking about Him either. You were just looking for another way to get over. You were just looking for another opportunity to get high. You were looking for another way to trick someone; looking for another man, another woman, another something to fulfill you. When God found you, you were not seeking God; you were somewhere spiritually asleep. But while you were sleeping, and while you were snoring, while you didn't have a care about God or His kingdom, God was saying, "I still want you, and I want you to be my house."

> God is saying, "I really love you and want to dwell in your house. I am going to live and dwell in you, and you are going to be my people, and I will be your God."

The thing I love about the God I serve is that He chose me while I was raggedy. He chose me while I was unfit. He chose me when I didn't deserve to be chosen. God doesn't have to do another thing for me, because He has done all that He needed to do when He forgave me and when He said that He would make me His tabernacle; when He said, "I really love you and want to dwell in your house. I am going to live and dwell in you, and you are going to be my people, and I will be your God."

How long was God hanging around your house before you let Him in? How long did God stand on the outside knocking on the door of your heart, pleading with you saying, "You don't feel like you need me, but I want you. You're still doing your own thing, but I want to dwell in

Building a Great House

you. I want to make you a temple, a living sanctuary, so that I can show forth My glory in your house!" Surely the Lord is in your place! Do you know what's going to happen to you before you finish this book? You're going to wake up out of your sleep, and you're going to say, "Surely the Lord is in this place!" I'm not talking about a physical building; I'm talking about your living tabernacle. *You* are the building. *You* are the temple of the Holy Ghost. *You* are the temple of Jesus. He lives and abides and dwells in you. Some of us need to wake up out of our sleep and say, "Surely the Lord is in this house, and this is a great house! Anywhere that the Lord has decided to reside has to be a great place." Even if your place is in need of improvement, it's still a great place; if the Lord moves into the house, He's going to fix that house. He will restore the house; He will rebuild and fix the house that you are, so that He can begin to fix houses around you.

Had Jacob known that the Lord was in that place, he would not have been scared of Esau; he would not have been roaming around looking for somewhere to go, because he would have known what the Lord said, and would have had confidence in the promises of God. God doesn't want you running from your challenges. Too many of us are running around the church shouting 'Hallelujah,' yet we're living defeated, broken down and raggedy lives. He is frustrated with stuff that does not bring edification and glorification to His name. He wants you to know that there's no

> *There's no obstacle you can't overcome; there's no situation that you can't deal with and there's no power that can stop you, because greater is He that is in you than he that is in the world!*

obstacle you can't overcome; there's no situation that you can't deal with and there's no power that can stop you, because greater is He that is in you than he that is in the world! You need to get ready to go where God told you you could go. Don't sit there and cry anymore. Don't make any more excuses. Determine to do something great! Stop whining about what you can't do. God wants you to get rid of all that defeated talk. God needs people that will say, "Bring it on! Bring whatever you feel like you need to bring, but whatever you bring won't stop me. You can't block me. When you block me to the right, I'm going to the left. You can't hold me back because I have greatness inside of me!"

> *Start dreaming once again about the goals you gave up on, and the things you quit on.*

Jacob was afraid and says, "This is none other but the house of God. This is the gate of heaven!" What God is showing us is that we don't have to wait to get to heaven to receive what God has for us. Heaven comes to you. You don't have to wait for the sweet by and by; get what God has for you right now! You can have it now, but you have to want it now. You have to stop taking leftovers, stop accepting hand-me-downs, and stop taking what folks throw at you. Just as God gave Jacob dreams, He has given you dreams, and all you need to do is get your dreams back! You need to start dreaming once again about the goals you gave up on, and the things you quit on. God told me to tell you, "If you don't give me a dream, I can't give you the power to fulfill that dream, but if you will give me a big dream, I'll show you a big deliverance!" (Keep in mind that deliverance does not always mean moving out from or away from something. It also means something being brought in, like your mail, pizza brought to your front door, or a package you were expecting.) Jacob saw in his dream angels descending and God said, "Not only am I going to make you great, and not only am I going to be with you, but I will send my angels to watch over, serve and assist you."

Now, you have God, The Holy Spirit, and the angels coming down to earth! What more do you need? All you have needed, God has provided; His name is Jehovah Jireh. His name is Jehovah Rohe. His name is Jehovah Tsidkenu. His name is Jehovah Shammah, and He lives on the inside of you and me! You can't bring me any sunshine because sunshine is in me. He is my sunshine on a cloudy day. If you have the Son on the inside, the clouds around you don't matter.

Take note that as soon as Jacob had a revelation that God had come down and that heaven had come down to visit him, he became aware of the awesomeness of God. It was the awesomeness of God that brought Jacob to the place where he understood that, early in the morning, it was time for him to worship. Once you realize who God is,

> *Once you realize who God is, you can't help but want a relationship with and long to worship Him.*

you can't help but want a relationship with and long to worship Him. So Jacob rose up early in the morning and built an altar, poured oil upon it, and made a sacrifice and a vow to the Lord. Jacob had to come to a place where he realized that God loved him so much that He was looking for a dwelling place in him. Jacob understood that if he was going to be great, he had to come into a covenant with Greatness. It was at that time that Jacob began to seek God on another level. Why? Because great people desire a more intimate relationship with God. God desires that same type of intimate relationship with you.

✘ Building a Great House ✘

My Personal Construction Site - 8

✘ I didn't recognize it at the time, but *this* was God!

_____

_____

_____

_____

_____

✘ My relationship with God is challenged in the following ways:

_____   _____

_____   _____

_____   _____

_____   _____

✘ Because I did not recognize God's presence, He and I wrestled with these things:

_____   _____

_____   _____

_____   _____

✖ I've learned to recognize God's presence by:

_____

_____

_____

✖ I am committed to developing my relationship with God through:

_____	_____
_____	_____
_____	_____
_____	_____

✖ This is what I sense God has said to me through this chapter:

_____

_____

_____

Nine

Characteristics
of
Great People

When you look at the characteristics of great people, you will notice these six traits:

- ❖ Great people are confident in who they are.
- ❖ Great people are conquerors.
- ❖ Great people are forward moving.
- ❖ Great people are envied by others.
- ❖ Great people become a blessing to others.
- ❖ Great people make others great.

Great Confidence

Do you know the person that God made you to be? Are you confident in the person that God made you, or are you still trying to find yourself? Do you know that you are the righteousness of God in Christ, and the head and not the tail? Or are you still trying to figure out who you are even though you have been saved for forty years? A great woman knows who she is and is secure in what she is, and so does a great man. Have you ever seen people who always need others to validate them? They have to be constantly told about their positive qualities. Every ten minutes they need to hear it; they need somebody to say something positive and uplifting about them, and if they don't get that, they suffer with self-esteem issues.

> *You can't allow yourself to be defined by other people's words. If you're going to be great, you have to become opinion-proof.*

If that describes you, let me tell you something; you need to get to the place in your spirit where you know who you are even if no other person says anything wonderful about you ever again. Stop this foolishness of waiting for someone to validate and agree with you about who you are. Guess what? People are never going to agree with you. As far as they are concerned, you're always going to be sorry. As far as they're concerned, they know what family you came from. As far as they're concerned, you'll never be good for anything, but you better know that you can't allow yourself to be defined by other people's words. If you're going to be great, you have to become opinion-proof. If you live your life based on other people's opinions, they're going to keep you small. They'll keep you cramped up in a box and won't let you get out. People like to look down on other people; it makes them feel good. They want to keep you small so that they can keep looking down on you. You'll be no bigger than a mustard seed when you let people define you.

You've got to know that you know who you are! God already knows who He is. I laugh to myself when people say, "God is going to prove Himself!" God is God whether He proves Himself or not. We've heard people say things like, "Lord if you heal me, I am going to know that You are God." He is God even if He doesn't heal you. When Jesus was brought before Pilate and the others who were going to crucify Him, the first thing they said was, "If you are the Son of God, show us some miracles. Let's see some of those miracles you worked. Let's see you heal somebody. Let's see you turn water into wine. Let's see you do some miracles!" Jesus didn't do a thing. What was Jesus saying to them? He was saying, "I don't have to prove anything to you. I am that I am." When you know who you are, when you really know who you are, you don't have to prove anything to anyone. Just be who you are. Be the best you can be. Do what you need to do so you can go where you need to go. You don't have to wait for anyone's approval. You don't have to wait until someone says you can. You have to know you can, whether someone tells you that you can or not. That's what is wrong with us now, sitting around waiting for somebody to tell us what we can do. You have to have this attitude: "Baby, even if you don't tell me I can do it, I can do it!" When you find out how great God is – and greater is He that is in you than he that is in the world – you will be able to look at anyone, even the devil and tell him, "You don't know who you are messin' with. I am great!"

Are you still defining yourself by your past problems? Don't allow people to define you and neither can you define yourself by things that have happened to you years ago, allowing your past to hold you back. Regardless of what your past has been, that is not all that you are or ever will be. People will tell you that you'll never be more than what they know your past to be. They will say things like "He ain't never gonna be nothing more than a drunkard; She will always be out there in those streets; He's been like that since I've known him and he will never get his act together."

> *Regardless of what your past has been, that is not all that you are or ever will be.*

People will always try to remind you of those skeletons in the closet, and sometimes the skeletons will try to break free and remind you themselves! But when you know who you are in Christ, then you know that you are a new creature, and old things are passed away; behold all things have become new.

You have to say to the world "You can't define me; you can't put a label on me. I know who I am so you can't tell me who I am. I don't live by your definition of me. You can't find a card in the card store that will describe who I am. You can get every big word, every nice word, and every deep word you can think of, but guess what? You can't describe me; I am indescribable. Who I am is just out of this world. I am beyond you." Be confident in who you are; be confident in your skills, talents, and abilities. When you get up in the morning after you slap those feet on the floor, with sleep still in your eyes and your hair all torn up, is run to the mirror and say, "Boy, you're great, because there's a great God inside of you. You are awesome; you're something else! You're too much! You got it going on; go 'head with your bad self!" You have to know that that attitude is not being cocky or arrogant; it's confidence. We have this confidence! We don't boast in ourselves, but we boast in the Lord. God didn't build any mess when He made you; God built something great.

✖ Building a Great House ✖

Great Conquerors

God has some great things for us to do and accomplish, and some of us haven't even gotten started yet. God develops us into conquerors and sets before us new territories to take over by His power. When God moves you to a place where there are others, He is not telling you to stay there with them. That's an indication that He's getting ready to move somebody out so He can move you in. In the sixth chapter of Joshua, when the Israelites took over Jericho, God gave them exactly what they needed in order to take the city. Jericho was a strong hold

> *When God moves you to a place where there are others, it's an indication that He's getting ready to move somebody out so He can move you in.*

but Jericho was a great city. There are Jerichos in your life, places that are built up, and mighty, but guess what? When God tells you to go there, He is getting ready to move the current inhabitants out. It was God's will for the Israelites to take the city of Jericho, regardless of its walls, its strengths, and its inhabitants. Understand that there are some places that God has destined you to go in your life, and your enemies may already occupy those places, but God is getting ready to evict somebody so you can move in. There is a great city already built up and prepared for you that He is getting ready to move you into, and in order to move you in, He has to move somebody out. The inhabitants can't stay there, because you're on your way. You need to tell them, "Move over. Greatness is coming through; I'm not coming to rent and I'm not coming to let you rule over me. I'm coming to take possession. I'm coming to get what belongs to me, and I don't mind fighting."

There are territories set for you to conquer; you see, there are some small people who are residing in your great city. God has allowed them to build the city, but when the inhabitants hear that you are coming, they will know that you aren't coming to play around! When God makes you great, He will make it so that your name and your reputation precedes you. When they hear that you are on your way, they will start to shut up all the windows and doors in an attempt to keep you from coming in. Rahab said to the Israelites, "We're in this walled city, but we are afraid! Your name has preceded you! We've heard about the plagues in Egypt and we've heard about the Red Sea. You all have made us nervous, because we heard about what you did to Pharaoh. We heard that Pharaoh brought all his chariots and all his armies to destroy you, but the God you serve told you to stretch out your rod, and the Red Sea opened up, and your people went through. When Pharaoh's people and all his chariots and all of his great men got into the Red Sea, God closed the curtain on Pharaoh. Now we're in here shaking and afraid, not sure about what to do and not sure how to act, because we know our time is coming!" Their city was shielded by walls that chariots could ride on, yet they were in there trembling. They were there taking B. C. Powder and nerve pills; they were shaken in that walled city. God will make it so that when your enemies hear your name, they will begin shaking in their boots. Don't you know that when you're great, God will scare your enemies to death? He will make the devil tremble. He will make the devil run. He will give the devil a heart attack.

✗ Building a Great House ✗

When you know that you know that God has sent you and has given you the land, you don't run from those enemies you have at work. You don't let those neighbors drive you out of your neighborhood. You don't let anyone take anything from you. Every day that you get up and go to your job, you should say, "Greater is checking in." They can have the devil, his mother and everyone else on the job, and they all want to get rid of you, but you have to know how bad you are. You have to have the attitude that you will not be moved, saying to yourself, "I am going to be here everyday with a smile on my face. You can do all your mess, but greater is here. The ditch you dig for me, you are going to fall into it. I will anoint your chair and this entire office and get you put out of here." They can't get rid of you when you know who you are. Those who don't know who they are in God say things like, "I'm going to change jobs, because these people are trying to get me fired." That's what the devil wants you to do;

> *When you've been in the presence of God, and you know who you are, just your very name will scare your enemies to death.*

he wants you to be a quitter. You have to tell the devil, "No; if God placed me here, He placed me here to succeed and not fail. If I leave, it's not going to be because of you, baby. If I leave, it will be because God told me to leave. If you think you and your raggedy self are going to run me out of something that God put me in, you can forget it, because I am a conqueror." When you know who you are, you never let them see you sweat. Don't ever let them see a wrinkle in your forehead. That is why you have to pray in the morning. If you're going into the devil's den, and you haven't prayed, fasted or worshipped, then everyday you'll be beat up, crying and saying, "I'm going to leave that job. They're trying to get rid of me!" But when you've been in the presence of God, and you know who you are, just your very name will scare your enemies to death. When you get into your prayer closet and get before the great God that you serve, and He starts telling you who you are and whose you are, and how much power He gave you, how much anointing is in your life, how much vision He put inside of you, and how big your dreams are, when He finishes with you and you go to work, everyone will say, "My God, greatness is here!" Don't you know that when you walk into a room, you're supposed to light it up? It doesn't matter how much darkness is in the room; you're supposed to light it up. You see, you're not great until you can tell the devil, "Sit down and watch this. I don't want you to go anywhere; sit here and watch all your plans fall apart. Sit here and watch the very one you tried to use to destroy me be destroyed; sit here and watch my enemies become my footstool." I have news for you; your enemies will fight the hardest when they know you are getting ready to win. When the battle gets hot, you know it's their last opportunity, and it's their last chance. There are some strongholds that the devil has been maintaining and telling you to keep out of. Don't you know there are some "No Trespassing" signs in your Jericho? But you have to tell the devil, "I'm coming in – not by my own power, but I'm coming in. I don't have any cannons. I don't have any weapons; the weapons of my warfare are not carnal but mighty through God." You have to say to yourself, "If I can hang in here through this one, then I have

> *Your enemies will fight the hardest when they know you are getting ready to win.*

it going on." Right where you are, with this book in your hand, you ought to shout "Glory!"

God instructed the people of Israel to first walk around the city, and God's command to you today, just as it was then to the Israelites, is that you walk around your Jericho walls and worship Him. You need to survey your territory; look at your city and how great its walls are. Look at the circumference of the land. Look at how powerful it is. God wants you to see it. Why? Because when God brings those walls down, you will know that it was not a fluke; it was not a wind, but it was God Almighty! Your victory will not come by power nor by might, but by the Spirit of the Lord. Look at those walls and know that God has given you the city. You don't even have to say anything; sometimes you can't say anything; you have to just look at what you are believing God for and say, "Lord, I trust and believe you."

> Your victory will not come by power nor by might, but by the Spirit of the Lord.

Can you imagine the anticipation of those Israelites on that last day of the march, on that seventh day – the day of God's perfect number? They stared marching around that wall and looking at that wall, trembling with excitement because they knew that the city was going to be delivered into their hands on that day. They didn't say much, but they could hardly contain themselves, because they knew God was getting ready to do something great. They were thinking, 'God is going to tear this city up! It belongs to us. Every deck, every house, everything in this city, God is getting ready to bless us with.' I can see them walking around, unable to say anything, but ready to shout "hallelujah!" They almost let a "Glory to

God" slip out. They had to slap their hands over their mouths to keep quiet. Sometimes when you know God is getting ready to do something great, you start acting funny, and people don't know what's wrong with you. Have you ever been in a situation where God has been so good to you that right in the middle of the grocery store, you had to contain yourself? Other shoppers saw you twitching and ready to burst at the seams and were wondering what was wrong with you. They didn't know that God was getting ready to do something great!

Those Israelites were quivering with so much excitement they could hardly stand it. They had to hold that excitement in, but at the end of that seventh time around, when they completed that final lap, God said, "Now you can shabach Me." Everything that they had built up on the inside, they let go in one great shout. When those walls fell, they rushed in, ready, and took the city!

Some of you have been quiet too long. You have been sitting around, bottled up and holding back too long. You have been quivering with excitement for too long. Right now, it's time for you to shabach God. You ought to shout, for God has given you the city. Watch those walls come falling down! God has given us what we need. God has given us what He said He would give us! Be ready to take the city. Don't you know that if you want to take something, you will have to fight for it? No one's going to just give you milk, and no one's going to just give you honey. You have to go in there and roll your sleeves up and tell them, "Greatness is here. Greater is He that is in me than he that is in the world, and I have come to get what belongs to me."

✚ Building a Great House ✚

Today if you're feeling small, if you're feeling defeated, if you're feeling like an outcast and that no matter what you do, it is never good enough, I want you to know that if you connect with God, He will evict your enemy, and He will bless you beyond your imagination.

Forward Moving

> *"Then Isaac sowed in that land, and received in the same year an hundredfold: and the Lord blessed him. And the man waxed great, and went forward, and grew until he became very great:"*
>
> *Genesis 26:12-13*

When you are going to be great, you always have to be moving forward. You can never be great backing up or standing there posing. Some people just pose, thinking they are cute, and just stand there like a manikin in the window of a store. They're not going backwards and they aren't going forwards; they're just standing there. You can't be great just standing there. Great people move forward. The Lord blessed Isaac and the man waxed great, but that wasn't all. He went forward and became *very* great. The Lord doesn't want you to be just great; He wants you to be very great! Move forward and onward. Don't settle for what you did yesterday; you have to want something if you're going to get something. Look for something to do and accomplish tomorrow. Strive for a better tomorrow.

Greatly Envied

> *"For he had possession of flocks, and possession of herds, and great store of servants: and the Philistines envied him. For all the wells which his father's servants had digged in the days of Abraham his father, the Philistines had stopped them, and filled them with earth.*
>
> *Genesis 26:14-15*

Great people understand that others will always envy them; look at the Philistines' reaction to Isaac's prosperity. The Philistines were upset because everything Isaac touched prospered; Isaac received a hundredfold return on what he had sowed. They did not want Isaac to prosper, so solely out of envy, they stopped up the wells. Let me remind you that not everyone wants you to be great, and out of their envy, they will try to stop you. They will try to sabotage what you already have going. Even though they filled the wells, that didn't stop Isaac. He didn't quit and cry because his water supply had been cut off. He still went forward! Great people don't cry when they lose something; there are great people all over the world that have lost fortunes and possessions over and over and over again. When you're great, you can lose all of your money, but you'll have it back soon, because the money didn't make you great; you made the money great. They know the same greatness that got it in the first place is able to get it again! They have lost all of their money and everything they had, but because greatness was on the inside of them, they didn't let what they lost stop them. When you're little, you let the loss of anything block you, stop you, make you depressed and mess up your party. The God you serve can take nothing and make something out of it, so it doesn't matter what you lose and who is envious, because if God be for you and if God is within you then what do you have to worry about? The Philistines stopped up the wells, but Isaac simply had new ones dug. He continued to honor God and continued to prosper. He wasn't shaken or deterred by the antics of those who were envious and jealous of his prosperity.

If you're going to be great, you'll have to learn how to deal with jealous people. You can't worry about people being jealous of you and what people are going to say; it will prevent you from moving forward. Why listen to somebody who's jealous and envious and doesn't want you to go anywhere? Why sit around and absorb that garbage? You are going to have to learn to say, "it's okay, you all can be jealous; The God I serve has made me great. I completely understand why your eyes are green with envy and red with anger." There will be people who won't like you just because you have it going on, whether you know it or not.

There are folks out there right now that are not speaking to you because they don't support your success. They don't want to deal with you anymore because they see you going somewhere, and they don't want to go. Every time you get ready to move up in the Spirit and get ready to prosper, here they come. If you aren't prepared to deal with that, instead of you moving on, you'll sit around crying and worried. "What is wrong with you?" "Lulu is not speaking to me anymore. She was my best friend. I don't know what happened." You can't let those negative attitudes intimidate and stop you. "She rolled her eyes at me; he's not speaking to me; I don't know what I did to make them not like me." So what? Who cares? You need to wipe those tears away and go on and be great despite what others are thinking and doing. Know that you are going to have to deal with people who will have that kind of attitude towards you. Say to those people, "I love you in Jesus' name, and I will pray for you; I'll help you if I can, but God knows I can't hang around here in this quicksand; I've got somewhere to go whether you like it or not."

Being a Great Blessing

Small people don't have the capacity to bless anybody; it takes somebody great to bless somebody else. When you have your palms upward, you operate as a receiver, waiting for someone to give you something and believing that it is the only way you can ever be blessed. But when you turn that hand over, your hand is not out for a blessing; you have become a blessing. Remember that great people are always looking for someone to bless. When you have great people in your church, they're not always worrying about what they're going to get, but they're always looking at how they can bless others. You should realize that people are blessed while you are sitting near them—simply because you are great, and because the God you serve is great. See, great people bring a blessing. God tells Abraham that He would make him a blessing; He doesn't say, "I want you to always have your hands stuck out, looking for a blessing." It's when you have a blessing in your hand that you know you're on your

> *Great people are always looking for someone to bless.*

Building a Great House

way to being great. When you have something that others can be blessed by, then you know you are becoming great because you are no longer the borrower, but you are the lender. You are no longer the receiver, but you have become the giver. Come to the understanding of what Jesus meant when He said it is better to give than to receive. Small people seek a blessing while great people have something to give. Have you ever seen anyone who always has his or her hand stuck out? Some of them live right in your house; they always need and are asking for something. They can never be great as long as their hands are stuck out. It's when you have something that God has blessed you with and you know it is more blessed to give than to receive, that you are on your way.

> *Don't limit your thoughts of being a blessing to just giving money.*

What is it that you have to offer to others to assist and bless them? Are you in a position to bless someone, or do you find that you are often on the receiving end? Don't misunderstand and limit your thoughts of being a blessing to just giving money. The Bible says in Acts that when the beggar asked Peter for money, his response was,

> *"Silver and gold have I none; but such as I have give I thee: In the name of Jesus Christ of Nazareth rise up and walk."*
>
> *Acts 3:6*

Didn't that man receive a great blessing? And guess what? God received glory from both the man that used to be lame, and from Peter. Peter, through the power of God, was the vehicle for the healing miracle that took place.

> *Take inventory of what you have to offer that will show forth the glory of God.*

Take inventory of yourself and what you have to offer that will show forth the glory of God, then determine to be a giver rather than a receiver.

Making Others Great

Just as every seed produces fruit after its own kind, great people produce great people. Let me remind you again of what Hebrews 3:3 says:

> *"He who hath builded the house hath more honour than the house."*

You've read earlier about the importance of having a mentor, now I want to stress to you the blessing it is in mentoring someone and building someone else up. It's glorious for you to become a Great House, but it is even more glorious when you build someone else up as a Great House. A lot of people talk about how great they are, but they're not building up anything or anybody; they aren't bringing anyone up with them. They aren't making any kind of impact. Realize that there are people around you who recognize who you are and what you are accomplishing, and strive to achieve the same level of success that you've been blessed to achieve. We hear people say all the time, "I want to be just like you when

�֍ Building a Great House �֍

I grow up." What they are really saying is, "I recognize that you are awesome; I see that you are doing something and going somewhere and I want to have that kind of impact!" Just as you had to sit at someone's feet to learn and be developed, there are others waiting to receive an impartation from you. You, as a great house, should develop those around you that desire to be great, into great houses! What good does it do you to suck everything up for yourself? How is God glorified in that? Great people have proteges and people that they mentor. They sow into the lives of those who want to draw from their strengths. They show another person what to and what not to do. When you build something great, that means you are greater, because what comes out of greatness is great, but that which produces greatness is always greater.

> *Just as you had to sit at someone's feet to learn and be developed, there are others waiting to receive an impartation from you.*

That's why no one can be greater than Jesus. He's always going to be King of kings and Lord of lords. Since He's the King of kings, then guess what you are? A king. You can't be the King of kings, but that does not mean that you are not a king. It means you are under Him. He's the first born among many brothers. Hebrews says He is the author and the finisher of our faith. That means He is the Alpha and the Omega. Not only did He start, but He also finishes. He which has begun a good work in you, shall keep it against that day!

The glory you get from building the house is automatically going to go to God. There is no need for you to be selfish, jealous or greedy because the man who builds the house is always going to get more glory than the house. When you bring up another man, you become greater and God is made greater even more so!

✘ Building a Great House ✘

My Personal Construction Site - 9

✘ I would rate my confidence level as:

_____
_____
_____
_____

✘ I would rate my intensity as a conqueror as:

_____
_____
_____
_____

✘ My ability to be forward moving can be proven by:

_____
_____
_____
_____

✘ There are some who envy me because:

_____
_____
_____

✘ I have blessed other people through:

_____
_____
_____

✘ My efforts to make others great have been:

_____
_____
_____

✘ This is what I sense God has said to me through this chapter:

_____
_____
_____

Ten

A Living Tabernacle

"Howbeit the most High dwelleth not in temples made with hands; as saith the prophet, Heaven is my throne, and earth is my footstool: what house shall ye build me? saith the Lord: or what is the place of my rest? Hath not my hand made all things?"

Acts 7:48-50

God's Search for a Dwelling Place

While God is building His church, He is building the people in the church. God is not as concerned about a physical building than He is the people inside the building. Many are building great big temples, but God is not concerned about big cathedrals; He is concerned about people. You see, sometimes, we get more caught up in the cathedral than we do the real temple. Rather than building brick and mortar structures, we should focus on building people. What good is it for man to build a great sanctuary if God doesn't have great sanctuaries in us? In order for God to build a Great House, He has to have men and women who are great houses.

God said to Himself, "I want a tabernacle, and I don't want it to be just any building; I want a building that can magnify me. I want a building that can worship me." So God made Himself a house and called his name Adam and whenever He came into the garden and Adam worshipped him, God heard himself in Adam. Whenever God would come down in the garden, it made God happy, because when He looked into Adam's eyes, He saw Himself. Whenever God saw Himself in His new house, He began to rejoice, because He could see His own glory in the image of the man He had made. Adam was the first tabernacle known on this earth as the house of God. Adam was the habitation of God. When Adam fell, God no longer dwelled in Adam, and when God no longer dwelled in Adam, then Adam could no longer dwell in the garden. When he fell to satan's temptation, Adam evicted God; he kicked God out of His house. Since that time, God has always been looking for a house - a man - to dwell in.

> *What good is it for man to build a great sanctuary if God doesn't have great sanctuaries in us?*

In the days of Moses, God would come down into the Holy of Holies once a year and visit his people. Although Moses had built Him a house, and it was a great house, it was not a permanent dwelling place. God could not inhabit the place, because it was not the temple He was looking for. It was just a place of visitation. It was just a temporary structure that He had Moses build in preparation for the real appearance He wanted to make. God did not want to dwell in a building. He did not want to dwell in a house fabricated of wood, stained glass and stone. God's spirit has never been able to dwell in a physical structure, but God longs to dwell in the spirit of man, the place He has chosen as His temple or tabernacle. But the tabernacle of Man must have the blood of the Sacrificial Lamb sprinkled on it and applied to it in order to cleanse it so that God's spirit can live inside.

The Tabernacle of Man

The whole time the Children of Israel were looking at the tabernacle, they were looking at God's living tabernacle, the make up of man - the body, soul and spirit. It is in comparing spiritual things with natural things that we are able to understand matters concerning our spirits. The outer court was the place where sins were offered up. In the spiritual, the outer court represents our flesh or is typical of our flesh, where we're still battling the sin nature of the first Adam who fell. The inner court had the table of showbread, the golden candlesticks and the table of incense; that bread represents the Word of God, and the candles represent the prayers of the saints. It is that second chamber, which is called the Holy Place that relates to the soul of man, that place where we think, that place where we deal with our humanity and the things that relate to this natural life as well as to the spirit. It is where the Word comes into us and transforms us by the renewing of our minds. It is the place where the revelation of the Word causes our minds to be transformed and changed, rather than being conformed to this world. When we understand that, then we can better understand that we pray not only out of our spirits, but also out of our souls, concerning the issues that affect us in our natural lives. So that two-fold thing, the soul of man and the flesh of man, has become the temple of God.

Once a year God would come down into the innermost court, or the Holy of Holies, which is symbolic of the spirit of man. In the natural, the innermost court is where the spirit of God came down and actually manifested His presence, where the priest would come in and sprinkle the blood on the Mercy Seat, and God would forgive His people of their sins on the Day of Atonement, that place of the Ark of the Covenant, which had the Ten Commandments carved in stone, the pot of manna and Aaron's rod that budded, even after it was disconnected from the tree. All of that is symbolic, in that Christ was being revealed from a natural perspective.

> Just as we have a natural house, we have a spiritual house, a spiritual tabernacle, in which the very nature and presence of God dwells.

We as spirit men, could not be effective in the natural earth without a natural house, so God gave us natural bodies in order to operate in the natural. We know the physical body is the house of the spirit; in the same way, our spirit must be the house of God's spirit. The spirit of a man has become the Holy of Holies, in which the spirit of God dwells. Just as we have a natural house, we have a spiritual house, a spiritual tabernacle, in which the very nature and presence of God dwells.

�֎ Building a Great House �֎

Knowing this, II Corinthians 4:6 begins to become clear as to what Paul meant when he wrote to the Corinthian church:

> *"For God, who commanded the light to shine out of darkness, hath shined in our hearts, to give the light of the knowledge of the glory of God in the face of Jesus Christ. But we have this treasure in earthen vessels, that the excellency of the power may be of God, and not us."*

Some translations talk about "pots of clay" in reference to earthen vessels. Everybody knows that man was formed from the dust of the earth. God scooped up clay, formed man, then breathed man's spirit into him, and that clay became a living soul. It's in this pot of clay, our natural man, that we have this treasure. What is the treasure in earthen vessels? That treasure is not only our spirit, but also the spirit of God dwelling in us.

> *We are a treasure in a clay pot. We are God's treasure.*

It is the spirit of man that makes this body alive; once the spirit leaves the body, the body deteriorates, earth to earth, ashes to ashes and dust to dust. In the same way that God is eternal, man's spirit is eternal. It lives on for eternity. You can't burn up a spirit or get rid of it; a spirit exists and remains throughout eternity. So when we talk about having that treasure in earthen vessels, then we are talking about the treasure of God's spirit, the glorious knowledge and the light and revelation of who He is, as it shines forth in our hearts. We are a treasure in a clay pot. We are God's treasure.

Deterioration of the Living Tabernacle

> *"Flee fornication. Every sin that a man doeth is without the body; but he that committeth fornication sinneth against his own body. What? Know ye not that your body is the temple of the Holy Ghost which is in you, which ye have of God, and ye are not your own? For ye are bought with a price; therefore glorify God in your body, and in your spirit, which are God's."*
>
> I Corinthians 6:18-20

Not only does God dwell in the Holy of Holies of our spirit, but He purchased and owns us totally, spirit, soul and body. The reality of it is, whether it's fornication, adultery or any other sin, when you commit those sins, you are, in fact, destroying the tabernacle of your body. You're destroying your physical, mental, and emotional man. Every sin defiles and hurts the temple. When you sin, you're doing damage that is sometimes hard to reverse because of the consequences of sin. You can destroy the temple.

Can God handle sin? Yes, God can handle sin, but man can't handle sin; this temple can't handle the cracks and the damage that result from sin. While God forgives sin, the damage you do to your soul and the damage you do to the temple in which God dwells, you can't handle. This body is not an issue with God because in the Holy of Holies there is forgiveness of sin. But what you have to understand is that, forgiveness does not necessarily repair the damage sin does to your physical life, your mental life, and your emotional life. Many times, even after God has come in to dwell within you, you have a hard time dealing with the damages of sin. Man is sin conscious. As long as you remain sin conscious, then that sin has an effect on you in the sense that it will condemn you; it will destroy you, and it will cause you to lose your ability to function properly in the kingdom of God. That's what people don't understand; God forgives you, but after God forgives you, you still have to live with yourself. You still have to sleep with yourself. Some of you are still living with the ghosts of your past and other situations that have damaged your temple. They have damaged your holy place. They have damaged the outer courts, and sometimes, although you are saved, if you don't allow God to heal you and to repair the damage that has been done in your soul, and in your spirit, you suffer the consequences of the damage for long periods of time.

There are many people who are saved, love Jesus and filled with the Holy Ghost, who still have cracks in their souls and in their lives. They themselves have done damage to the temple and are still struggling with the effects of the damage today, even though God is living on the inside. It's the sin that you do without, that affects the God within. Because of that damage, you become limited in your capacity to allow God to do in you what you need Him to do. You have to understand the penalty of sin; the fact that you can do a lot of damage to your temple does not mean you can't be saved, but it does mean that you may never come into your greatness, and into your full potential because of the damage you've allowed to be done in your life that you haven't been able to overcome.

The only way you are going to be a great habitation is to get and embrace the revelation that you are the sanctuary of God. God Himself walks and lives inside of you, and if He lives inside you, then His nature, His image, His power, His glory and the manifestation of His presence should be reflected in you. The God that is in you should be seen on the outside. What you do, and how you respond to the presence of God, and what you accomplish, reflects your attitude towards your temple, and the fact that God resides in your temple.

> *Embrace the revelation that you are the sanctuary of God.*

The Corporate Body

> *"And we are built upon the foundation of apostles and prophets, Jesus Christ himself the chief corner stone; in whom all the building fitly framed together groweth unto an holy temple in the Lord, in whom ye also are builded together for an habitation of God through the Spirit."*
>
> Ephesians 2:20-22

Again, when God builds a Great House, He has to have great people. Now when you read this particular text, you notice that rather than focusing on your personal temple as an individual, it focuses on the universal church or

"The Body of Christ." This is the greater tabernacle that God Himself is building. Not only are we as individuals temples of God, but also collectively as a corporate body, we are the house of God. God is in you, the individual, but there also is a place where God comes in corporately. It takes all of those great people together, in the spirit of God, functioning and being built in God's purpose and plan, to bring God the glory that He wants from a universal church and from The Body of Christ as a whole. He dwells in The Body that has been "fitly framed together," that The Body might function as it is supposed to. The Body, functioning properly, will bring God glory.

The Purpose of The Body

God builds this greater tabernacle because He desires to impact creation in its entirety. Ephesians 4:8 says that when Jesus ascended, He led captivity captive and He gave gifts unto men. We have to understand that when He gave these ministry gifts to men, He gave them apostles, prophets, evangelists, pastors and teachers that they might perfect, or

> *Wherefore he saith, When he ascended up on high, he led captivity captive, and gave gifts unto men.*
> *Ephesians 4:8*

mature the saints for the works of the ministry (Ephesians 4:11-12). Most of us don't really understand the purpose of the five-fold ministry. Most people who come in contact with it don't like it, because its purpose is not to entertain you; it's to build you and make you. Anybody can be entertained, but if you are going to be built and made into what God intends for you to be, it's going to take sacrifices. It is going to take some going through. The role of the apostle, the prophet, the evangelist the pastor, and the teacher is to be God's ambassadors to build up, train and develop the church, and cause it to arrive at a place of maturity. Paul as an apostle, said he was a master builder, called to build, impart into and raise up the body of Christ for the purposes of God. That title doesn't apply just to Paul; God wants all of His people to be wise master builders, not just builders, but wise master builders. The sad part is, the church body today does not want to be built up the right way. We want to be great in our own way. When you become great your way, your house is not going to stand. People want to build big natural buildings, but they don't want to deal with themselves. They don't want to be "under construction." You're a big construction site (somebody should just put a sign on your head, which reads "God at work"). God wants to build you into a Great House, but you have to cooperate! Instead of being built, we want to be played with. "Just entertain us," we say. "Tickle us, and make us feel good. We'll come to your church; we'll give you money; just make us happy. This is happy hour!" Realize that God did not come for a happy hour visitation; He came to make a habitation within us.

God is not finished with The Body; The Body is not yet complete. There is still much work that needs to be done on this corporate building. So God continues to use the ministry gifts within us, if they function properly, to be the tools or the vehicles through which He builds the

> *God continues to use the ministry gifts within us, if they function properly, to be the tools or the vehicles through which He builds the church.*

church or corporate body. If we are going to be great in God, we must allow God to build us. We are the sanctuary that God is investing in and wants to build for His glory.

My Personal Construction Site - 10

🛠 My thoughts on allowing God to dwell in me:

____

____

____

____

____

🛠 Although God has forgiven me, I've caused damage to my temple by:

____________________ ____________________

____________________ ____________________

____________________ ____________________

____________________ ____________________

🛠 I am allowing God to repair my temple by staying committed to Him through:

____________________ ____________________

____________________ ____________________

____________________ ____________________

✹ Building a Great House ✹

✹ I am committed to building the Body of Christ by:

_____

_____

_____

✹ This is what I sense God has said to me through this chapter:

_____

_____

_____

Eleven

The Tabernacle Sacrificed

"For it is not possible that the blood of bulls and of goats should take away sins. Wherefore when He cometh into the world, He saith, Sacrifice and offering thou wouldest not, but a body has thou prepared me: in burnt offerings and sacrifices for sin thou hast had no pleasure."

Hebrews 10:4-6

A Worthy Sacrifice

The Israelites knew that they could come up to God once a year and offer up rams, goats and lambs as sacrifices for atonement, but while they could be forgiven, they still had to live with their consciences and the penalties of sin, because there was no redeemer. That animal sacrifice was only a type of forgiveness, and it was as if God "winked" at their sins because of that sacrifice. God accepted the burnt offerings but He wasn't well pleased with them. These sacrifices and burnt offerings were not the best. He no longer wanted the blood of goats and bulls. He desired a permanent sacrifice. What was the will of God? That Jesus be the eternal sacrifice. When Jesus came, it was to permanently redeem us from, and to destroy the consequence and the penalty of sin. Because Jesus could not have redeemed us without a body, He had to become the temple of God that would be offered up for all of the rest of the temples that God would raise up and indwell. Jesus, understanding that animal sacrifices could no longer suffice and were not satisfactory to redeem men from their eternal damnation, agrees to become a worthy and perfect sacrifice.

> *Wherefore when he cometh into the world, he saith, Sacrifice and offering thou wouldest not, but a body hast thou prepared me:*
> *Hebrews 10:5*

Jesus could not become the perfect sacrifice as long as He remained in Heaven on the right hand of the Father. He could not become the perfect sacrifice until God prepared Him a house of flesh so that he (Jesus) could become the house of God. Jesus didn't come as a ghost; He came in a body of flesh, and that body had to be offered up in order for us to receive redemption. In other words, man's redemptive status in God was just temporary, because all of those bulls, goats and rams were just temporary remedies to an eternal problem. That kind of sacrifice was just a temporary thing God used and accepted until He was ready to bring in an eternal solution. What was the eternal solution? The Lamb of God, God's secret weapon, who was in His bosom, was already prepared and already sacrificed. It was the Lamb that was slain.

We fail to understand that what we saw at Calvary was something that had already taken place in God. What we put in time, God already had in eternity. It happened two thousand years ago according to our calendar, but in God, Calvary happened before the foundation of the world. Therefore, Calvary shows us that when God decides to do something, it is so even before it manifests. That is why He can say that the Lamb was slain before the foundation of the world, because when God decided to do it, it was done. God insisted that He was going to have a temple, a Great House, and God insisted that He was going to build this Great House. To ensure that He was going to have this Great House, anything that might hinder that Great House from being built, He stopped in Himself before it ever started. In other words, before sin ever came into being, there was a Lamb already slain before the foundation of the world. So in God, there is no time; in God there is no season. We are the ones who are messed up by time. The Lamb was eternal in God.

God's Eviction and Reinstatement

We've already discussed that when God made Adam, God wanted to visit with Adam; God wanted to dwell in and have a habitation in Adam. God was in Adam but then Adam, through his disobedience evicted God out of His house, and as a result God evicted Adam from the garden. It was a spiritual eviction; you see, it was not God who evicted Adam, but Adam evicted God.

The natural eviction that Adam suffered was the manifestation of a spiritual eviction that God suffered. What God did to Adam seems to be bad, but what Adam did to God was worse. You can do without the garden if you have God, but when God is gone, what good is the garden? When God is in you, you can be in the desert and turn the desert into a garden. When God is in you, you can turn death into life. When God is in you, you can turn that which is sick into something that has been healed, and you can turn poverty into prosperity. It doesn't matter what conditions I find myself in, because when greatness is there, my circumstances have to change. But when a man gains the whole world and God is gone, what good is it?

> *God was in Adam but then Adam, through his disobedience, evicted God out of His house.*

It was God who was evicted out of Adam's temple, so God had to reverse the plan. In the same way that man was lost, he had to be won. The same thing that the enemy did to Adam in the garden, God had to do, in reverse, in Jesus. When Jesus came, He came to reverse the loss that Adam took in the garden so that we could regain what Adam lost. God didn't come to save angels; God came to save man. So if He was going to save man, He had to save man by man. There is one mediator between God and man, and that is The Man, Christ Jesus. Now, Adam was the first tabernacle in the earth that God actually indwelled, and, until Jesus, he was the last. This is why Jesus was so strange to common men, because Jesus was the first person they had ever seen who actually had God in Him as a habitation. Before Jesus, the prophets, Noah and all the other great men of God that came down through time never saw themselves as the tabernacle of God. God visited Enoch. God visited Moses. They had encounters and experiences with God, but they were never the habitations of God. They had times and seasons when they met with God. They had some aspect of God and saw dimensions of God, but they were never the dwelling place of God. They couldn't be the dwelling place, because the temple of man was contaminated by sin and needed the blood of the Sacrificial Lamb. What the Pharisees and Saducees and other religious folks saw in Jesus was life, and what they saw in their religion was death.

> *Once Jesus sacrificed His temple, He redeemed man from sin and made it once again possible for God to dwell in the house of His choice, man!*

God inside of Jesus was greater than their religion. When God didn't look like their religion, it blew their minds. So when Jesus came with life and life more abundantly, they experienced an overload. That's why they saw Jesus as an "alien" or a "freak;" religious people couldn't handle Jesus.

Once Jesus sacrificed His temple, He redeemed man from sin and made it once again possible for God to dwell in the house of His choice, man! Jesus died then was buried, and while Jesus' body was in the earth, His body was a seed that God invested in the earth. God did not want just that one body; He wants bodies. Once we have been washed and cleansed by the blood of the Lamb, our houses become available to be filled with the Spirit of God. We are able to welcome God in.

God is still looking for bodies. God is saying to us today as a church, "Prepare me a body that I can glorify myself through." He's saying, "Prepare me a vessel that I can use, that I can live in, that I can be myself in. Prepare me a body that I can magnify myself in. Prepare a body in which I can be glorified."

The body must be prepared. The Body is supposed to be prepared, in that it is being put through a process whereby God can use it, and God can show Himself mighty in our lives.

The Glorified Temple

After his death and burial, Jesus didn't throw His body away. Jesus didn't say, "Okay, I hung on the cross, died, and was buried, snatched the keys of death, hell and the grave, and now I don't need this body anymore. Ashes to ashes and dust to dust." That was not the case. That body, which was necessary for our redemption, had to be resurrected; Jesus had to come back in that same body. In the same way He left in that body, He is going to return in that body. As a matter of fact, in Psalms, David declared that Jesus' body would not see corruption. How? Because God was going to raise up that temple in three days. When Jesus made that statement to the religious leaders of that time, they thought that He meant the natural temple, the one that took forty-eight years to build, but that was not the temple He was talking

> *Jesus saith unto her, Touch me not; for I am not yet ascended to my Father: but go to my brethren, and say unto them, I ascend unto my Father, and your Father; and to my God, and your God.*
> *John 20:17*

about. He was talking about raising His own temple. The glory of God was going to be manifested to man through that temple.

The Bible says this Lamb that was slain, rose again on the third day, and when Mary Magdalene came to touch him, He said, "Don't touch me." He couldn't be touched because if He had been touched, His temple would have been contaminated. He had to first take His temple up before God, to have it preserved for eternity (John 20:17). When He came back to His disciples, He then allowed them to touch Him. He had returned in the flesh; a ghost doesn't have flesh and bones. He said, "Thomas, touch Me; handle Me. Am I not the same one that you all buried? You don't believe it; you think that I'm a ghost." Then a resurrected Jesus ate fish and honeycomb; we all know that ghosts don't eat. Jesus is not some spirit. Now He had flesh that all of a sudden appeared in a room, but His disciples still could touch Him. The Bible says the same way you saw Him go up, is the same way He's going to return. Every eye shall see Him and we shall be just like Him. Every one that condemned Him, every eye and every tongue shall confess that Jesus Christ is Lord to the glory of the Father. When everybody sees Him, they will see the wounds in His hands and feet. He will say, "I'm that same Jesus that you all crucified; the same Jesus that you all buried and said was gone."

In the same way, God is going to raise your temple up, then breathe your spirit back in it, so that you'll have immortality for the rest of your life. If we are going to be just like Jesus, we have to have a glorified body. Those who are dead in Christ are not going to stay dead, but they are going to rise again. They will have been buried with Christ, and they shall be raised with Christ. Those who are alive and remain shall be changed in a moment, in a twinkling of an eye, and mortal shall put on immorality. Won't it be something when God goes back and gets every fiber of your being, puts it together, glorifies it, puts your spirit back in it, and you stand up into who you are, but in an immortal body? You'll have the same glorified body that Jesus had when He came back to visit His disciples! Thank God for a glorified body! Oh death where is your sting? Oh grave, where is your victory?

✗ Building a Great House ✗

My Personal Construction Site - 11

✗ Have I served God an eviction notice through my disobedience?

_____

_____

_____

_____

✗ Because of Christ's redemptive work at Calvary, have I welcomed God into my life, His temple?

_____

_____

_____

_____

✗ This is what I sense God has said to me through this chapter:

_____

_____

_____

Conclusion

This Great House I've been talking about can be your own life. Once you find out who you are, whose you are, and who is in you, then it will change the very mentality and attitude by which you embrace God. Most Christians act as if they belong in the junkyard, because they don't have the revelation of God in them. Is God in you? Are you His tabernacle? Are you going to be a Great House that God dwells in? Haggai 2:7-9 says,

> *"And I will shake all nations, and the desire of all nations shall come: and I will fill this house with glory, saith the Lord of hosts. The silver is mine, and the gold is mine, saith the Lord of hosts. The glory of this latter house shall be greater than of the former, saith the Lord of Hosts: and in this place will I give peace, saith the Lord of hosts."*

God says that the glory of the latter house shall be greater than that of the former house. The glory of this latter house, the New Testament church, the body of the church that God is building not made with hands, shall be greater than the former house. God is building us up to exceed the glory of the former house. God is still looking for bodies through which He can magnify Himself. Are you going to be a part of His building process? This house shall be the greater house, the latter house, the Great House.

✴ ✴ ✴

You may have just finished this book and you recognize that you are in your Egypt, or maybe you are journeying through your wilderness, or simply realize that you have not yet come into the greatness that you desire and that God has destined you for. You can never be great until you meet this great God that I have shown you through this book. You will never reach your greatest potential without the Lord Jesus in your life and in your heart. I want you to know that He cares about you. He wants you to be great, and He longs to dwell within your temple. Let Him in today by praying this simple prayer:

> *Father God,*
> *You loved me so much, that You gave Your only begotten Son to be offered as a living sacrifice to die for my sins so that I would not perish, but would have everlasting life. Your Word says that we are saved by grace through faith as a gift from You. There is nothing that I can do to earn salvation. I believe in my heart and*

confess with my mouth that Jesus Christ is Your Son and that He died on the cross for me and bore all of my sins, paying the price for them. I believe that You raised Jesus from the dead. I ask you to forgive me of my sins. I confess Jesus as my Lord. According to your Word, I am saved and will spend eternity with You. I invite you into your new home and I am thankful that you chose me to dwell in. Thank you Lord.

In Jesus' Name, Amen.

⚒ ⚒ ⚒

If you just prayed this prayer and received Christ in your life as your personal Savior, let me be the first to congratulate you and welcome you to the body of Christ. You have made an awesome and powerful decision, the best decision you will ever make! I personally want to hear from you and invite you to email me at info@fgkc.com. Also, be sure to visit the Full Gospel Kingdom Church either online, at www.streamingfaith.com, pointing your browser to the Full Gospel Kingdom Network, at www.fgkc.com, or in person at Full Gospel Kingdom Church - 3114 Washington Avenue, Newport News, VA 23607.

God Bless You!
Bishop Felton Hawkins

⚒ ***End***

Coming in 2006!

Congratulations! Your house has been completely restored, remodeled and renovated. It's come a long way in the process, and it is a structure that both you and God can truly be proud of. But . . . are you ready to be the man of your house – the woman of your house?

Since the beginning of time, God has placed responsibility on the shoulders of a man, not only giving him dominion over every living thing on the earth, but also giving him specific instructions to take care of it all. Today, man still has that same charge, but what happens when a man shuns that responsibility? What happens when that man fails to uphold and maintain his position in the difficult times he's faced with today?

In the time and day we are now living, the enemy has been successful in deceiving thousands of women to believe that they must fight for their equality with man. In their desire to obtain their rights as women, many have strived to be equal with man in every facet of life, and have attempted to compete on every front. This has caused an earthquake at the very foundation of the family and has brought on a spirit of rebellion, not against man, but against God. Can a woman be whole within herself as a wife, mother, and minister in her home?

Man of the House – Woman of the House

Get ready to take dominion!

Felton Hawkins

ISBN: 0-9721623-2-1 - Publication Date: Summer 2006

Bishop Felton Hawkins is the founder and Senior Pastor of Full Gospel Kingdom Church, in Newport News, Virginia. He has persisted in building a principle-based body of believers through his teaching and preaching over the past twenty years.

Bishop Hawkins is a powerful teacher and expositor on the subject of leadership pertaining to the Body of Christ. He is the founder and president of Empowered For Impact Ministries (EFIM). As such, he partners with pastors throughout North America, teaching and preaching leadership development to their congregations and fulfilling the EFIM purpose: empowering believers to become leaders in the kingdom of God.

Because of his integrity and powerful message, Bishop Hawkins is constantly sought after to speak to congregations and facilitate leadership seminars and conferences. He is rapidly grasping the attention of pastors and ministry leaders and is the founder and overseer of the Kingdom Covenant Churches, which encompasses eight congregational ministries.

His weekly television program, Empowered for Impact, airs on the PAX network reaching thousands of television viewers, and millions worldwide can view his ministry online at www.streamingfaith.com. He resides in Virginia with his wife, Sylvia, and three children.